BR STEAM MOTIVE POWER DEPOTS

LMR

Paul Bolger

IAN ALLAN
Publishing

Preface

Introduction

The purpose of this book is to assist the average enthusiast be he modeller, relic collector or historian, with his search for information on Motive Power Depots — the home of the steam locomotive.

Many devotees will recall the experience of touring such an establishment; the hiss of steam, the clank of engine movements and the sight of smoke suspended from the ceilings above the many varieties of engine in different stages of repair.

The sight of a fully serviced locomotive simmering outside the Depot on a crisp bright morning is a memory I shall never forget. I hope that the following pages aid the reminiscences of those fortunate enough to have lived during the steam age.

The book is dedicated to my uncle, Thomas Smythe, who, in the 1960s unselfishly devoted much of his spare time to help me pursue my schoolboy interest in the steam engine.

Paul Bolger

For reasons of space the depots covered by this work have been restricted to those which possessed a code, as these were the venues which were visited most often by enthusiasts and were of the greatest importance to the railway network in general.

In all, 126 depots are outlined and for continuity of the text the codes used for the headings are, in the majority, c1950. As many codes altered with the change of regional boundaries, certain sheds which spent the major part of their BR existence in other regions as sub-sheds have qualified for inclusion in this volume — The London Midland Region. Examples of these sheds are 4C Swansea Upper Bank, 13E Upminster and 29C Dundee West (see Notes).

Acknowledgements

This book has been made possible with the invaluable help of the following people and organisations: Mr T. J. Edgington of the National Railway Museum; Mr G. Goslin of the Gresley Society; Mr J. B. Hodgson of the Lancashire and Yorkshire Society; Mr J. C. James of the London and North Western Society; Mr G. M. Kitchenside of Locomotive & General Railway Photos; Mr A. C. Macleod of the Railway Correspondence & Travel Soc; Mr K. Montague of the British Rail Public Reglations Dept; Miss S. Percy of the Ordnance Survey; Mr Rhodes of Real Photographs; Mr C. Turner of Photomatic; Mr H. N. Twells of the London Midland & Scottish Society.

Special thanks are due to the following for their assistance in tracing the photographs and maps within the book: M. Bentley; H. C. Casserley; G. Ellis; B. Hilton; F. Lyon; W. Potter; and Mrs Mowah, Miss O'Donoghue, Mr Jones and their colleagues at the British Museum Map Library.

In addition, grateful thanks are extended to the following: C. A. Appleton; N. Ashfield; R. Blencowe; R. Carpenter; D. Carville; C. Clark; T. David; F. Dean; M. Dunnett; R. J. Essery; C. I. K. Field; V. Forster; J. Gilmour; M. Hale; L. Hanson; P. H. Hanson; D. Hardy; G. Heywood; I. G. Holt; M. S. Houlgrave; R. T. Johnson; N. Joseph; B. C. Lane; A. W. Martin; B. Morrison; T. Nicholls; C. H. S. Owen; J. Page; J. A. Peden; N. E. Preedy; G. Reeve; D. Rendell; F. W. Shuttleworth; N. Skinner; J. D. Stevenson; M. R. Stubbs; W. Stubbs; J. Thomlinson; T. Thompson; S. G. Underwood; J. R. Walker; J. Wilden; A. Willis; T. Wright.

In the course of preparation the following publications were of major importance as reference and consultative material: *The Railway Observer* (Volumes 20 to 38); *The Railway Magazine* (Volumes 94 to 114); *Railway World* (Volumes 19 to 29); *Trains Illustrated* and *Modern Railways* (Volumes 3 to 21).

Errata

p5 (1B) closed 1962, coded 1B 1948-1962
p46 (8E) coded 13E 1949-1950, 8E 1950-1958
p50 (9C) origin North Staffordshire Railway
p52 (9E) coded 13A 1949-1950, 9E 1950-1956
p54 (9F) coded 13C 1949-1950, 9F 1950-1956
p55 (9G) coded 13D 1949-1950, 9G 1950-1958
p62 (10F) coded 13G 1949-1950, 10F 1950-1952
p71 (12E) origin Furness Railway
p106 (21C) coded 85D 1960-1964
p109 (22B) coded 85C 1960-1964
p132 (26G) coded 13B 1949-1950, 26G 1950-1955
p137 (27E) coded 13F 1949-1950, 27E 1950-1963

First published 1981
Reprinted 1993

ISBN 0 7110 1019 6

Published by Ian Allan Ltd, Shepperton, Surrey. Phototypeset and printed by Ian Allan Printing Ltd at their works at Coombelands in Runnymede, England.

Notes about Contents

The group of sheds from 4B to 4E, although of LMS vintage, were administratively transferred to the BR Western Region at the outset of nationalisation in 1948. However, arising from indecision over districts and code numbers the actual groups did not appear until 1949 in the form of 81A onwards. It must, therefore, be argued that until the new codes were issued the depots would have been operating under the ex-LMS codes (4B to E) with the London Midland Region controlling, albeit in a caretaking capacity. It is largely with this in mind that these four depots have been included.

This is not the case with 4A Shrewsbury which was the only depot in the group to have been owned jointly by the GWR and LNWR. Although the ex-LMS (LNWR) side of the site retained its 4A code until 1949, the shed became the sole responsibility of the Western Region in this year using the code 84G. Because of the original part GWR ownership and the length of its service in the Western Region this depot will be included in that volume to avoid duplicity.

13A Plaistow, 13C Tilbury, 13D Shoeburyness and the ex-LMS Scottish sheds (27A Polmadie to 32C Forres, except 29C Dundee West) have not been included as their major service was with the Eastern and Scottish Regions respectively from 1949 and all received codes of their own within those areas. 13E Upminster and 29C Dundee West only survived as sub-sheds in the said regions which is why they have been catered for in this volume. 13B Devons Road is the exception to both rules as it became 1D, thus spending its full BR lifetime within the London Midland Region.

Whilst, at first, it seems contradictory to include the bulk of the (four) group for one reason and to exclude the (13) and Scottish groups for another, it must be remembered that strict compliance with the coding system would have resulted in severe duplication of the contents of this and the volumes that will follow, particularly with the Eastern and Scottish Regions. A balance has, therefore, been struck in an attempt to combat the effects of BR's failure to issue each region with its codes in January 1948. It is hoped that the resulting regional 'limbo' where it occurs will not hinder your enjoyment of the book.

Pre-Grouping Origins

Although, primarily, not relevant to the period covered, an indication of the vintage of the shed is given by the inclusion of the company of ownership prior to 1923. This is not necessarily the company which commissioned the building, as many smaller installations were absorbed into the larger companies by the takeover or amalgamation of district railways.

Gazetteer References

These numbers refer to the page and square within the Ian Allan's *Pre-Grouping Atlas* which pinpoint the subject's national location.

Closing Dates

The dates given indicate the closure of the depot to steam engines only. However, in some cases the date would have been the same for diesels where the building closed completely, either as a result of its dilapidated condition or the effects of the 'Beeching' cuts.

Shed Codes

British Railways chose to adopt the ex-LMS system of coding depots for all of its six regions. This method of locomotive identification dated from 1935 and the London Midland Region's use of them from 1948 to 1968 was, in the main, a continuance of those existing at the end of the LMS in 1947 (Groups 1 to 28). The codes used during these years are, therefore, included together with the period of occupation. Where the last date of shed-code occupation does not coincide with the closing date of the depot, this is due to the shed having been demoted to sub-shed. This was most common when the depot was earmarked for closure or if the duties were considerably reduced. However, exceptions did occur; eg: Market Harborough, which was promoted to 2F in 1955 from the rank of sub-shed. The engine's smokebox carried a small oval plate bearing the code of its home depot (see page 141).

Allocations

Where the depot's lifetime allows, three separate allocations, of steam locomotives only, are listed from the years 1950, 1959 and 1965. There are a few exceptions to these years but they are confined to the minor sheds. The main lists are accurate to September 1950, March 1959 and April 1965. It will be seen that the power classification abbreviations for certain classes were altered between the years.

Plans

With the exception of the following depots: 2C, 2E, 4D, 9C, 9D, 10A, 11D, 12B, 12C, 13E, 14C, 15A, 15B, 15D, 16B, 21C, 23B, and 25C, all the plans have been based upon the Ordnance Survey County Series and National Grid maps from various years and have been reproduced by permission of The Controller of Her Majesty's Stationery Office, Crown Copyright Reserved.

Photographs

It has not been possible to restrict the views of all the depots to the period 1948/68 but this does not impair the overall presentation of any one shed greatly.

1A WILLESDEN

Pre-Grouping Origin: LNWR
Gazetteer Ref: 39 C3
Closed: 1965
Shed-Codes: 1A (1948-1965)
Allocations: 1950

Class 3MT 2-6-2T

40004	40018	40052	40073	40135
40006	40044	40054	40081	40204
40009	40046	40055	40087	40206
40017	40050	40072	40109	

Class 4MT 2-6-4T

42117	42118	42316

Class 5MT 2-6-0

42747	42787	42817	42885	42940
42786	42812	42870	42931	

Class 4F 0-6-0

44116	44372	44442	44497
44208	44381	44451	

Class 5MT 4-6-0

44833	45024	45041	45089	45146
44875	45025	45064	45097	45353
44911	45027	45071	45140	

'Patriot' 4-6-0

45509

'Jubilee' 4-6-0

45591 *Udaipur*
45625 *Sarawak*

Class 2MT 2-6-0

46431	46432	46433

Class 3F 0-6-0T

47342	47412	47475	47520	47676
47361	47430	47491	47531	
47380	47474	47505	47675	

Class 8F 2-8-0

48011	48310	48476	48624	48656
48122	44312	48551	48626	48657
48129	48327	48557	48628	48658
48147	48340	48600	48629	48659
48171	48354	48601	48632	48660
48172	48368	44602	48633	48665
48174	48416	48603	48634	48679
48278	48433	48605	48648	48758
48309	48438	48610	48649	

Class 7F 0-8-0

49021	49117	49163	49277	49344
49062	49122	49164	49296	49356
49078	49139	49275	49342	

Class 2F 0-6-0

58280	58285	58302
58283	58286	58303

Total 135

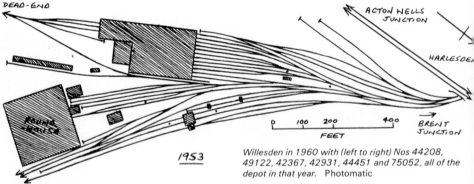

1953

Willesden in 1960 with (left to right) Nos 44208,
49122, 42367, 42931, 44451 and 75052, all of the
depot in that year.   Photomatic

Class 3 2-6-2T

40003	40019	40045	40051	40066
40007	40042	40046	40053	40068
40010	40043	40047	40060	40069
40016	40044	40050	40064	40070

Class 4 2-6-4T

42117	42351	42368	42489	42604
42118	42359	42422	42538	42611
42234	42360	42430	42576	42627
42304	42365	42463	42579	
42321	42366	42482	42585	
42350	42367	42487	42586	

Class 6P5F 2-6-0

42747	42852	42870	42931	42975
42812	42859	42885	42944	

Class 4F 0-6-0

44058	44208	44451
44116	44372	44497

Class 5 4-6-0

44771	44916	45187	45350	45381
44838	45024	45278	45372	45387
44869	45027	45288	45374	45404
44875	45064	45324	45375	

'Patriot' 4-6-0

45500 *Patriot*
45510
45511 *Isle of Man*
45547

'Jubilee' 4-6-0

45603 *Solomon Islands*
45740 *Munster*

Class 2 2-6-0

46424	46458

Class 3F 0-6-0T

47315	47482	47486	47559
47412	47483	47501	

Class 8F 2-8-0

48036	48325	48551	48629	48665
48074	48335	48600	48632	48729
48122	48416	48601	48648	48764
48129	48440	48603	48649	
48134	48476	48624	48656	
48171	48518	48628	48657	

Class 7F 0-8-0

49070	49122	49277	49413
49078	49164	49344	

Total 130

Allocations: 1965

Class 4MT 2-6-4T

42071	42105	42222	42431	42611
42080	42106	42233	42577	42616
42096	42114	42287	42581	
42102	42118	42289	42583	

Class 4MT 2-6-0

43007	43018

Class 5MT 4-6-0

44661	44833	44865	45331
44760	44844	44985	45379
44774	44860	45292	45393
44780	44862	45299	45418

Class 2MT 2-6-0

46507	46508	46509	46512

Class 3F 0-6-0T

47432	47435

Class 8F 2-8-0

48036	48518	48601	48624	48658
48347	48531	48603	48628	48754

Class 4MT 2-6-0

76035	76037	76039	76041

Class 2MT 2-6-0

78018	78033	78038	78060
78019	78034	78039	78063
78029	78035	78043	

Total 67

1B CAMDEN

Pre-Grouping Origin: LNWR
Gazetteer Ref: 39 B5
Closed: 1961
Shed-Code: 1B (1948-1961)
Allocations: 1950

'Patriot' 4-6-0

45514 *Holyhead*
45522 *Prestatyn*
45532 *Illustrious*
45541 *Duke of Sutherland*

'Jubilee; 4-6-0

45601 *British Guiana*
45669 *Fisher*
45672 *Anson*
45676 *Codrington*
45735 *Comet*
45736 *Phoenix*

'Royal Scot' 4-6-0

46100 *Royal Scot*
46101 *Royal Scots Grey*
46116 *Irish Guardsman*
46118 *Royal Welch Fusilier*
46126 *Royal Army Service Corps*
46139 *The Welch Regiment*
46140 *The King's Royal Rifle Corps*
46141 *The North Staffordshire Regiment*
46142 *The York & Lancaster Regiment*
46148 *The Manchester Regiment*
46151 *The Royal Horse Guardsman*
46152 *The King's Dragoon Guardsman*
46154 *The Hussar*
46159 *The Royal Air Force*
46162 *Queen's Westminster Rifleman*
46168 *The Girl Guide*
46170 *British Legion*

Turbomotive 4-6-2

46202

'Coronation' 4-6-2

46237 *City of Bristol*
46238 *City of Carlisle*
46239 *City of Chester*
46240 *City of Coventry*
46241 *City of Edinburgh*
46242 *City of Glasgow*

Looking east towards the western end of the shed in 1958, with 'Jubilee' class No 45630 Swaziland and 'Coronation' class No 46247 City of Liverpool in the foreground. The building was demolished in 1964. B. Hilton

1B CAMDEN 1951

'Coronation' 4-6-2 continued
 46244 *King George VI*
 46245 *City of London*
 46247 *City of Liverpool*
 46249 *City of Sheffield*
 46250 *City of Lichfield*
 46251 *City of Nottingham*
 46252 *City of Leicester*
 46253 *City of St Albans*
 46256 *Sir William A. Stanier FRS*
 46257 *City of Salford*
Class 3F 0-6-0T

47254	47359	47527	47668
47356	47467	47529	47669
47358	47522	47667	47671

Total 56

Allocation: 1959

'Patriot' 4-6-0
 45514 *Holyhead*
 45522 *Prestatyn*
 45523 *Bangor*
 45532 *Illustrious*
'Jubilee' 4-6-0
 45592 *Indore*
 45601 *British Guiana*
 45606 *Falkland Islands*
 45669 *Fisher*
 45676 *Codrington*
 45686 *St Vincent*

 45722 *Defence*
 45735 *Comet*
'Royal Scot' 4-6-0
 46100 *Royal Scot*
 46139 *The Welch Regiment*
 46144 *Honourable Artillery Company*
 46146 *The Rifle Brigade*
 46154 *The Hussar*
 46161 *King's Own*
 46162 *Queen's Westminster Rifleman*
 46168 *The Girl Guide*
 46170 *British Legion*
'Coronation' 4-6-2
 46229 *Duchess of Hamilton*
 46239 *City of Chester*
 46240 *City of Coventry*
 46242 *City of Glasgow*
 46245 *City of London*
 46247 *City of Liverpool*
 46254 *City of Stoke-on-Trent*
 46256 *Sir William A. Stanier FRS*
Class 3F 0-6-0T

47302	47529
47304	47668
47307	47669
47310	47671
47348	
47495	
47514	
47522	

Total 41

6

1C WATFORD

Pre-Grouping Origin: LNWR
Gazetteer Ref: 11 G1
Closed: 1965
Shed-Code: 1C (1948-1965)
Allocations: 1950

Class 3MT 2-6-2T
40010   40020   40043
Class 2P 4-4-0
40672
Class 2MT 2-6-2T
41220
Class 2P 0-4-4T
41908   41909
Class 4MT 2-6-4T
42119   42159   42378   42589   42598
42120   42178   42389   42590
42121   42304   42468   42593
Class 4F 0-6-0
44441   44443
Class 3F 0-6-0T
47355
Class 7F 0-8-0
48915   49157   49375
49145   49323   49393
Class 2F 0-6-0
58272

Total 30

Allocations: 1959

Class 2P 4-4-0
40672
Class 2 2-6-2T
41223   41224*
Class 2P 0-4-4T
41901
Class 3F 0-6-0
43325
Class 4F 0-6-0
44348   44440   44442
Class 2 2-6-0
46431
Class 3F 0-6-0T
47355

Class 4 2-6-4T
80034   80036   80038   80065   80067
80035   80037   80064   80066   80068

Total 20

*In 1960, No 41224 was thought to be the last remaining loco on the LMR with the early BR livery 'British Railways'.

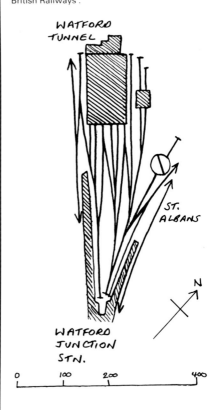

The shed in 1962, from the station. Photomatic

Devons Road in 1952 (looking south). This depot was the first all diesel shed in the country losing its steam classes in 1958. W. Potter

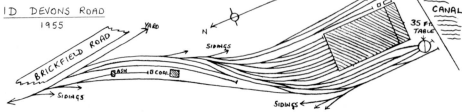

1D   DEVONS ROAD

Pre-Grouping Origin: North London Railway
Gazetteer Ref: 40 C3
Closed: 1958
Shed-Codes: 13B (1948-1949)
1D (1949-1958)
Allocations: 1950 (1D)

Class 4F 0-6-0
44348   44370
Class 3F 0-6-0T
47302	47487	47514
47304	47488	47515
47306	47489	47516
47307	47490	47517
47310	47492	47518
47312	47493	47558
47314	47494	47559
47315	47495	47560
47348	47497	47561
47349	47498	47564
47350	47499	
47411	47500	
47482	47501	
47483	47506	
47486	47511	

Class 2F 0-6-0T
| 58852 | 58853 | 58855 | 58858 | 58859 |

Crane Engine 0-4-2ST
58865

Total 48

2A   RUGBY

Pre-Grouping Origin: LNWR
Gazetteer Ref: 10 A4
Closed: 1965
Shed-Codes: 2A (1948-1963)
1F (1963-1965)
Allocations: 1950 (2A)

Class 4P 4-4-0
| 41090 | 41122 | 41165 |
| 41105 | 41152 | 41174 |

Class 4MT 2-6-4T
| 42155 | 42541 | 42577 | 42673 |
| 42487 | 42576 | 42585 | |

Class 4F 0-6-0
| 44058 | 44392 | 44456 |
| 44354 | 44395 | |

Class 5MT 4-6-0
44710	44860	45000	45187	45404
44711	44862	45002	45250	45419
44712	44863	45003	45282	45429
44713	44866	45004	45372	45430
44714	44867	45020	45374	45431
44715	44870	45033	45375	45441
44716	44909	45034	45379	45493
44831	44910	45092	45391	
44836	44915	45150	45394	

Class 2MT 2-6-0
46459

Class 3F 0-6-0T
| 47360 | 47378 | 47379 | 47677 |

8

The depot in 1954 looking west. The rebuilding of the shed commenced in 1955. W. Potter

WORKS

SCALE

0   100   200   400

N

CLIFTON MILL

T.T.

RUGBY MIDLAND STN.

CLIFTON MILL

Class 8F 2-8-0
48039	48320	48427	48509
48085	48343	48437	48559
48165	48372	48479	48729
48173	48398	48505	48736

Class 7F 0-8-0
49392	49411	49416	49431	49452
49398	49413	49423	49433	
49408	49415	49425	49447	

Class 1P 0-4-4T
58083

Class 2F 0-6-0
58181   58269

Total 98

Allocations: 1959 (2A)

Class 4P 4-4-0
41162

Class 2 2-6-2T
41214   41278

Class 2P 0-4-4T
41902   41909

Class 4 2-6-4T
42061	42541	42577	42673
42062	42573	42669	

Class 4F 0-6-0
44064   44395

Class 5 4-6-0
44711	44833	44863	44909	45493
44715	44836	44866	44915	
44716	44860	44867	44938	
44831	44862	44870	45146	

Class 2 2-6-0
46420	46446	46472

Class 3F 0-6-0T
47269

Class 8F 2-8-0
48012	48131	48365	48526	48757
48018	48136	48423	48559	
48035	48173	48427	48646	
48085	48203	48437	48668	

Class 7F 0-8-0
49245	49266	49377	49442

Class 2F 0-6-0
58199	58218	58308

Total 59

Allocations: 1965 (1F)

Class 5MT 4-6-0
44715	44771	44836	45001	45113
44716	44831	44866	45065	45448

Class 8F 2-8-0
48365	48445	48526	48559

Total 14

2B NUNEATON

Pre-Grouping Origin: LNWR
Gazetteer Ref: 16 F5
Closed: 1966
Shed-Codes: 2D (1948-1950)
2B (1950-1963)
5E (1963-1966)
Allocations: 1950 (2B)

Class 3MT 2-6-2T
40201   40202   40205   40208
Class 2P 4-4-0
40413   40438   40447   40508   40528
Class 2MT 2-6-2T
41234   41235   41236   41237   41238

Class 5MT 2-6-0
42777   42783   42814   42932   42941
42781   42813   42888   42933   42944
Class 5MT 2-6-0
42960
Class 4MT 2-6-0
43020   43022   43024
43021   43023   43025
Class 4F 0-6-0
44352
Class 3F 0-6-0T
47285   47286   47367   47594
Class 8F 2-8-0
48016   48036   48077   48526   48723
48020   48061   48345   48716
Class 7F 0-8-0
48927   49318   49396   49429   49451
49068   49339   49397   49432   49453
49181   49350   49414   49434
49186   49368   49418   49435
49304   49385   49424   49436
Class 3F 0-6-0
52141   52322   52429   52465
Class 2F 0-6-0
58118   58240

Total 73

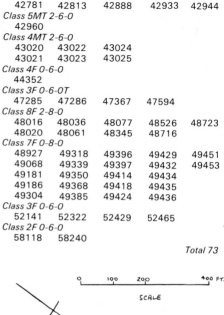

2B NUNEATON
1954

The shed in 1954, looking south. A start was made on rebuilding in 1957. In 1960 the depot received five unrebuilt 'Patriots' for light duties, namely

Nos 45533, 45537, 45538, 45541 and 45548.
W. Potter

Allocations: 1959 (2B)

2C NORTHAMPTON

Class 3 2-6-2T
40087	40135	40157	40207
40104	40138	40204	

Class 6P5F 2-6-0
42781	42783	42817	42891

Class 4 2-6-0
43000	43003	43020	43026
43001	43005	43023	43034
43002	43007	43024	

Class 3F 0-6-0T
47285	47594

Class 8F 2-8-0
48016	48258	48345	48456	48723
48020	48312	48398	48623	48751
48077	48320	48435	48658	
48154	48343	48449	48686	

Class 7F 0-8-0
48927	49142	49293	49414	49431
49002	49144	49314	49415	49432
49112	49181	49342	49425	49440
49120	49270	49350	49430	49441

Total 62

Allocations: 1965 (5E)

Class 2MT 2-6-0
46430	46459	46495	46520

Class 8F 2-8-0
48054	48174	48289	48456	48718
48074	48206	48320	48504	48751
48111	48263	48343	48650	48753
48154	48264	48386	48686	

Class 5MT 4-6-0
73004	73038	73045	73096
73032	73039	73048	73159
73033	73040	73073	

Class 4MT 4-6-0
75016	75045	75052

Total 37

*Looking east towards Northampton shed in 1965,
the year of closure.* W. Potter

Pre-Grouping Origin: LNWR
Gazetteer Ref: 10 B2
Closed: 1965
Shed-Codes: 2C (1948-1950)
4B (1950-1952)
2E (1952-1963)
1H (1963-1965)
Allocations: 1950 (4B)

Class 2P 4-4-0
40412	40421	40653
40420	40534	40657

Class 2 2-6-2T
41218	41219

Class 4F 0-6-0
44072	44076	44387	44491

Class 5MT 4-6-0
45021	45091	45191	45331

Class 1P 2-4-2T
46666

Class 3F 0-6-0T
47299	47318	47612

Class 8F 2-8-0
48422	48426	48550
48423	48445	48693

Class 7F 0-8-0
48914	49153	49270	49321	49366
48936	49203	49271	49357	

Class 2F 0-6-0
58218	58281

Total 37

Allocations: 1959 (2E)

Class 2 2-6-2T
41218	41219	41320

Class 4 2-6-4T
42353	42615

Class 3F 0-6-0
43399

11

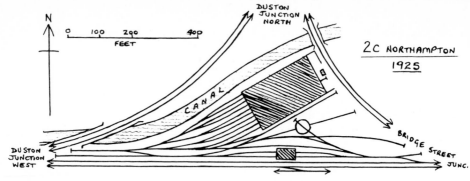

DUSTON JUNCTION NORTH

N

CANAL

BRIDGE STREET JUNC.

DUSTON JUNCTION WEST

0 100 200 400
FEET

Class 4F 0-6-0
44076 44242 44391 44524
44219 44353 44491

Class 5 4-6-0
44712 45147 45237 45392
45050 45191 45292 45409
45091 45222 45307

Class 3F 0-6-0T
47318 47499

Class 8F 2-8-0
48090 48269 48305 48422 48493
48147 48290 48360 48445 48534

Class 7F 0-8-0
49105

Total 37

Allocation: 1965 (1H)

Class 2MT 2-6-2T
41218 41219

Class 5MT 4-6-0
44869 45134 45308 45398
44936 45287 45349 45426
45051 45302 45392 45454

Class 3F 0-6-0T
47286 47499 47590

Class 8F 2-8-0
48020 48147 48349 48449 48739
48134 48247 48440 48506

Total 26

2D COVENTRY

Pre-Grouping Origin: LNWR
Gazetteer Ref: 10 A5
Closed: 1959
Shed-Codes: 2F (1948-1950)
2D (1950-1959)
Allocations: 1950(2D)

Class 2MT 2-6-0
46445 46446

Class 7F 0-8-0
49330 49441 49444
49405 49442 49446

Class 2F 0-6-0
58217 58278 58293 58306

Total 12

LEAMINGTON JUNCTION

N

0 100 200 400 LEAMINGTON
FEET

The depot (looking north) in 1950. The shed roof was renewed in 1957. Upon closure the engines transferred to Nuneaton, Rugby and Birkenhead.
LGRP courtesy David & Charles

The depot in 1954 with Class 8Fs on view. The full title of the shed was Warwick Milverton, upon closure the locos went to Leamington (Western Region 84D). W. Potter

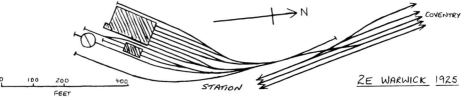

2E WARWICK 1925

2E WARWICK

Pre-Grouping Origin: LNWR
Gazetteer Ref: 10 B5
Closed: 1958
Shed-Codes: 2E (1948-1950)
2C (1950-1958)
Allocations: 1950(2C)

Class 3MT 2-6-2T
40002   40076   40078   40203
Class 2MT 2-6-2T
41227   41228   41239
Class 4MT 2-6-4T
42671   42674
Class 1P 2-4-2T
46683   46749
Class 8F 2-8-0
48012   48018
Class 7F 0-8-0
49430
Class 2F 0-6-0
58290   58308

Total 16

2F MARKET HARBOROUGH

Pre-Grouping Origin: LNWR
Gazetteer Ref: 16 G2
Closed: 1965
Shed-Codes: 2F (1955-1958)
15F (1958-1960)
Allocations: 1959(15F)

Class 4 2-6-4T
42446
CLass 4F 0-6-0
44388
Class 7F 0-8-0
49444   49447

Total 4

Looking west to the shed in 1960 showing the overhead water tank arrangement. Whilst previously a sub-shed of Rugby, this depot acquired its own code in 1955 but, in 1960, it lost this status and became a sub-shed once again, this time under 15A Leicester Midland. M. S. Houlgrave

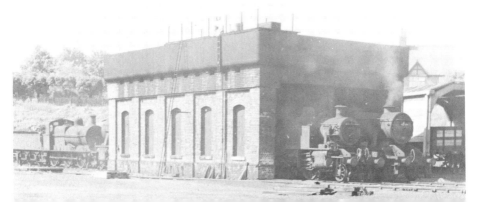

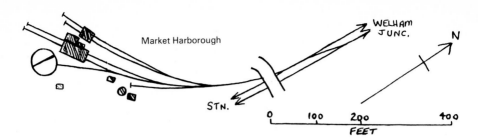

Market Harborough

WELHAM JUNC.

N

STN.

0 100 200 400

FEET

3A BESCOT

Pre-Grouping Origin: LNWR
Gazetteer Ref: 15 F4
Closed: 1966
Shed-Codes: 3A (1948-1960)
21B (1960-1963)
2F (1963-1966)
Allocations: 1950(3A)

Class 5MT 2-6-0
42779 42853 42894
42851 42891 42929
Class 5MT 4-6-0
44914 45310 45417 45433
Class 2MT 2-6-0
46425 46426 46427
Class 3F 0-6-0T
47382 47396 47519

Class 8F 2-8-0
48120 48318 48335 48518 48674
48175 48325 48375 48556 48686
Class 7F 0-8-0
48905 49063 49106 49245 49328
48907 49071 49114 49246 49334
48917 49077 49142 49265 49354
48950 49081 49180 49266 49359
49009 49089 49189 49282 49361
49022 49093 49202 49308 49367
49025 49096 49216 49313 49371
49045 49099 49223 49327
Class 2F 0-6-0
58257 58277

Total 67

Allocations: 1959(3A)

Class 3 2-6-2T
40080 40083 40173
Class 2P 4-4-0
40673 40692

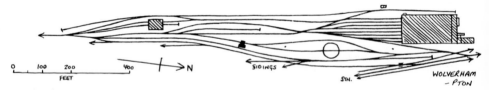

SIDINGS
STN.
N
0 100 200 400
FEET
WOLVERHAMPTON

The shed in 1960, looking north towards Classes 8F
and 7F locos. The rebuilding of this shed began in
1951. W. Potter

3A BESCOT 1938

Class 6P5F 2-6-0
42779   42782   42853   42921
Class 3F 0-6-0
43189   43760   43822
Class 4F 0-6-0
44448   44488   44512
Class 5 4-6-0
44873   45051   45385
44914   45114   45419
Class 2 2-6-0
46421   46425   46459   46490
Class 3F 0-6-0T
47294   47349   47382   47396
47296   47354   47385   47474
Class 8F 2-8-0
48250   48477   48705   48733   48769
48310   48514   48713   48755
48366   48556   48722   48762
48375   48602   48725   48766
48453   48674   48727   48767
Class 7F 0-8-0
48930   49077   49216   49313   49373
48964   49099   49246   49327   49387
49021   49106   49275   49328
49045   49114   49278   49343
49063   49125   49308   49361
Class 2F 0-6-0
58122   58169   58174   58181   58283

Total 81

Allocation: 1965(2F)

Class 4MT 2-6-0
43002   43005
Class 4F 0-6-0
44057   44155   44210
44139   44188   44377
Class 5MT 4-6-0
44766   44914   45067   45288
44840   45048   45089   45324
44875   45064   45222   45493
Class 2MT 2-6-0
46421   46429   46456   46522
46425   46445   46490   46527
Class 3F 0-6-0T
47437

Class 8F 2-8-0
48101   48478   48674   48725   48766
48256   48514   48680   48726   48767
48335   48522   48705   48729   48769
48366   48529   48713   48733
48375   48556   48719   48747
48477   48659   48724   48752
Class 4MT 2-6-0
76036   76047   76087
76042   76086   76088

Total 62

3B   BUSHBURY

Pre-Grouping Origin: LNWR
Gazetteer Ref: 15 F3
Closed: 1965
Shed-Codes: 3B (1948-1960)
21C (1960-1963)
2K (1963-1965)
Allocations: 1950(3B)

Class 3MT 2-6-2T
40047   40049   40053   40066
Class 2MT 2-6-2T
41225
Class 4F 0-6-0
44027   44439   44492
Class 5MT 4-6-0
45287   45405   45434   45437
'Patriot' 4-6-0
45524 Blackpool
45545 Planet
'Jubilee' 4-6-0
45703 Thunderer
45718 Dreadnought

A 1958 view with Class 2F No 58119 of the shed in
the centre. By this year the shed roof had
deteriorated somewhat and was in need of repair.
W. Potter

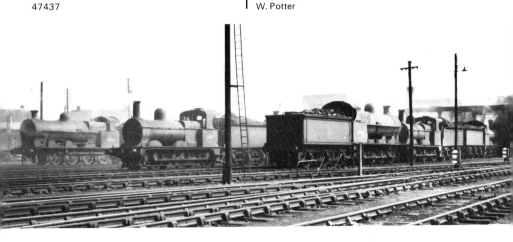

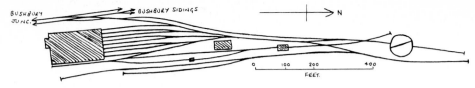

BUSHBURY JUNC.

BUSHBURY SIDINGS

N

FEET.

3B BUSHBURY 1947

'Jubilee' 4-6-0 continued
45722 Defence
45724 Warspite
45726 Vindictive
45733 Novelty
45741 Leinster
45742 Connaught
Class 3F 0-6-0T

| 47397 | 47398 | 47399 | 47473 |

Class 7F 0-8-0

| 48902 | 49037 | 49162 | 49196 | 49240 |
| 48940 | 49044 | 49167 | 49204 | 49346 |

Class 2F 0-6-0

| 58119 | 58152 | 58287 | 58368 | 58378 |

Total 41

Allocations: 1959(3B)

Class 2 2-6-2T

| 41225 | 41279 |

Class 4 2-6-4T
42428
Class 4F 0-6-0

| 44027 | 44439 |

Class 5 4-6-0

| 44829 | 45287 | 45395 | 45439 |
| 45015 | 45310 | 45405 |

'Jubilee' 4-6-0
45555 Quebec
45647 Sturdee
45688 Polyphemus
45709 Implacable
45734 Meteor
45737 Atlas
45738 Samson
45741 Leinster
45742 Connaught

Class 3F 0-6-0T

| 47363 | 47397 | 47398 | 47473 |

Class 7F 0-8-0

| 48950 | 49044 | 49411 |
| 49037 | 49240 | 49452 |

Class 2F 0-6-0

| 58118 | 58124 | 58204 | 58295 |
| 58119 | 58183 | 58281 |

Total 38

3C WALSALL

Pre-Grouping Origin: LNWR
Gazetteer Ref: 15 F4
Closed: 1958
Shed-Code: 3C (1948 to 1958)
Allocations: 1950 (3C)

Class 3MT 2-6-2T

| 40011 | 40019 | 40045 |

Class 2P 4-4-0

| 40462 | 40501 |

Class 2MT 2-6-2T
41226

An interior view of the depot in 1955 with LNWR Webb Class 1P No 46712 and 'Black Five' No 45308, both of Walsall. It will be seen that the shed had lost its roof by this time. Upon closure the locos and men were divided between Bescot and Aston.   J. Bentley collection

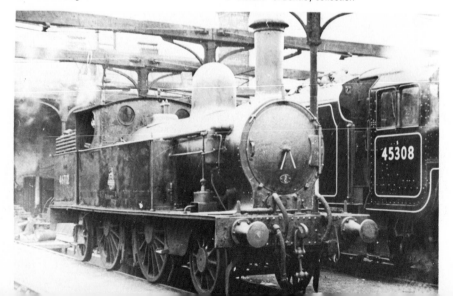

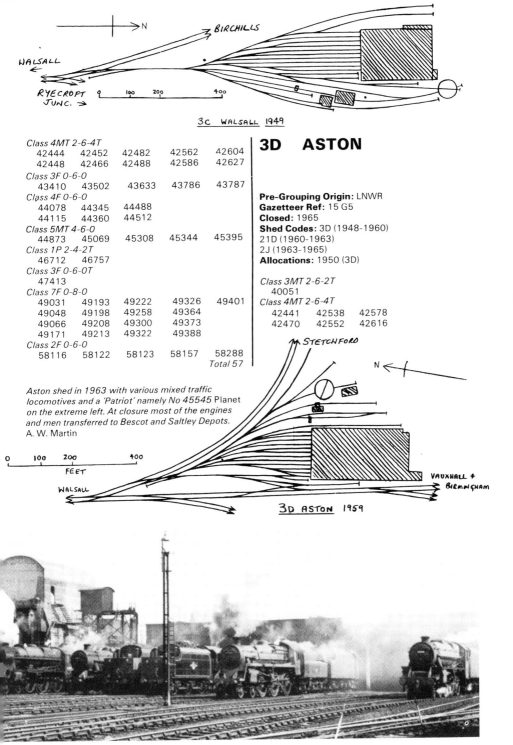

3C WALSALL 1949

Class 4MT 2-6-4T				
42444	42452	42482	42562	42604
42448	42466	42488	42586	42627

Class 3F 0-6-0				
43410	43502	43633	43786	43787

Class 4F 0-6-0		
44078	44345	44488
44115	44360	44512

Class 5MT 4-6-0				
44873	45069	45308	45344	45395

Class 1P 2-4-2T	
46712	46757

Class 3F 0-6-0T
47413

Class 7F 0-8-0				
49031	49193	49222	49326	49401
49048	49198	49258	49364	
49066	49208	49300	49373	
49171	49213	49322	49388	

Class 2F 0-6-0				
58116	58122	58123	58157	58288

Total 57

3D ASTON

Pre-Grouping Origin: LNWR
Gazetteer Ref: 15 G5
Closed: 1965
Shed Codes: 3D (1948-1960)
21D (1960-1963)
2J (1963-1965)
Allocations: 1950 (3D)

Class 3MT 2-6-2T
40051

Class 4MT 2-6-4T		
42441	42538	42578
42470	42552	42616

Aston shed in 1963 with various mixed traffic locomotives and a 'Patriot' namely No 45545 Planet on the extreme left. At closure most of the engines and men transferred to Bescot and Saltley Depots. A. W. Martin

3D ASTON 1959

Class 5MT 2-6-0
| 42782 | 42921 |

Class 5MT 2-6-0
42946	42951	42958	42973
42947	42954	42963	42974
42948	42957	42966	

Class 3F 0-6-0
| 43308 |

Class 4F 0-6-0
| 44061 | 44302 | 44490 |
| 44219 | 44350 | 44517 |

Class 5MT 4-6-0
44872	45052	45322	45446
44942	45058	45349	45448
45051	45094	45397	

Class 3F 0-6-0T
| 47363 | 47364 | 47365 | 47366 |

Class 7F 0-8-0
| 49017 | 49140 | 49261 | 49370 |

Class 2F 0-6-0
| 58117 | 58182 | 58279 |
| 58180 | 58185 | 58295 |

Total 52

Allocations: 1959 (3D)

Class 3 2-6-2T
| 40180 | 40206 |

Class 4 2-6-4T
| 42470 | 42552 | 42616 | 42658 |

Class 6P5F 2-6-0
| 42920 | 42929 | 42940 |

Class 6P5F 2-6-0
| 42947 | 42951 | 42957 | 42974 | 42979 |

Class 4F 0-6-0
| 44120 | 44302 | 44492 | 44517 |

Class 5 4-6-0
44844	44942	45132	45353	45448
44872	45058	45231	45370	
44876	45065	45322	45418	
44897	45094	45349	45430	

Class 2 2-6-0
| 46423 | 46427 | 46492 |

Class 8F 2-8-0
| 48718 | 48719 | 48726 | 48752 |

Class 2F 0-6-0
| 58182 |

Total 43

Allocations: 1965 (2J)

Class 4MT 2-6-4T
| 42062 | 42066 | 42069 | 42075 | 42604 |

Class 5MT 4-6-0
44710	44942	45058	45322	45439
44859	45038	45114	45405	
44872	45052	45310	45430	

Class 2MT 2-6-0
| 46427 | 46492 |

Class 4MT 2-6-0
| 76040 | 76095 |

Total 22

3E   MONUMENT LANE

Pre-Grouping Origin: LNWR
Gazetteer Ref: 13 C3
Closed: 1962
Shed-Codes: 3E (1948-1960)
21E (1960-1962)
Allocations: 1950 (3E)

Class 4P 4-4-0
| 41111 | 41116 | 41151 | 41172 |

Class 4MT 2-6-4T
| 42262 | 42264 | 42267 | 42489 |
| 42263 | 42265 | 42469 | 42579 |

Class 3F 0-6-0
| 43231 |

Class 4F 0-6-0
| 44057 | 44361 | 44506 | 44514 | 44592 |

Class 5MT 4-6-0
| 44829 | 45015 | 45390 | 45418 |

Class 2MT 0-6-2T
| 46900 | 46912 | 46922 |

*The depot in 1953 (looking west). At closure the
locos and men went to Aston.   B. Hilton*

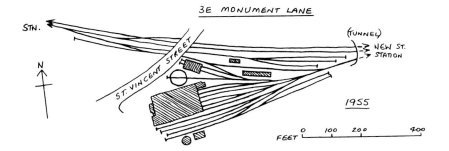

STN.

(TUNNEL)
NEW ST. STATION

ST. VINCENT STREET

N

1955

FEET 0 100 200 400

Class 2F 0-6-0
| 58124 | 58178 | 58273 |
| 58177 | 58179 | 58307 |

Class 2F 0-6-2T
58928

Total 32

Allocations: 1959 (3E)

Class 3 2-6-2T
| 40108 | 40118 | 40129 |

Class 4P 4-4-0
| 40936 | 41168 |

Class 4 2-6-4T
| 42267 | 42488 | 42601 | 42674 |

Class 4F 0-6-0
| 43973 | 44115 | 44490 | 44514 |
| 44057 | 44444 | 44506 | |

Class 5 4-6-0
| 44807 | 45034 | 45052 | 45308 |
| 44840 | 45038 | 45071 | |

Class 3F 0-6-0T
| 47494 | 47561 |

Class 2F 0-6-0
| 58178 | 58185 | 58220 |

Total 28

The entrance of Bletchley depot in 1960 with two of its 'Black Five' allocation Nos 45331, 45388 on display. The ex-LNWR roof was renewed in 1953. W. Potter

---

4A   BLETCHLEY

Pre-Grouping Origin: LNWR
Gazetteer Ref: 10 D2
Closed: 1965
Shed-Codes: 2B (1948-1950)
4A (1950-1952)
1E (1952-1965)
Allocations: 1950 (4A)

Class 2MT 2-6-2T
41222

Class 4MT 2-6-4T
| 42303 | 42446 | 42591 | 42659 | 42669 |
| 42348 | 42566 | 42600 | 42666 | |

Class 4MT 2-6-0
| 43000 | 43002 | 43004 |
| 43001 | 43003 | 43005 |

Class 4F 0-6-0
| 43841 | 44447 |

Class 5MT 4-6-0
44864	45057	45316
44865	45130	
44916	45314	

Class 1P 2-4-2T
46601

Class 3F 0-6-0T
| 47288 | 47298 | 47452 | 47521 |

19

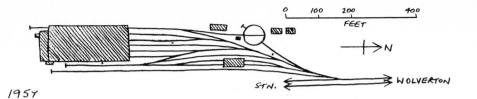

1954

STN. ← ⟶ WOLVERTON

Class 7F 0-8-0

48951	49014	49154	49292	49443
48952	49049	49155	49307	49448
48953	49061	49173	49391	
48964	49070	49287	49406	
49005	49088	49288	49417	
49007	49144	49289	49427	

Class 2F 0-6-2T

58897	58908	58926

Total 59

Allocations: 1959 (1E)

Class 2 2-6-2T

41222	41275

Class 4 2-6-4T

42467

Class 4F 0-6-0

43841	44364	44397
44072	44370	44447

Class 5 4-6-0

45020	45184	45331	45393
45089	45195	45388	

Class 3F 0-6-0T

47500	47521

Class 8F 2-8-0

48207	48535	48549	48610	48754
48446	48544	48550	48688	

Class 7F 0-8-0

48898	49061	49287	49403
48951	49093	49289	49443
48953	49094	49310	49450

Class 4 4-6-0

75030	75036	75037	75038	75052

Class 4 2-6-4T

80039	80042	80081	80084
80041	80043	80082	80085

Class 2 2-6-2T

84002	84004

Total 54

Allocations: 1965 (1E)

Class 4MT 2-6-0

43017	43073	43122

Class 5MT 4-6-0

44837	44870	44915	45027
44863	44909	44938	

Class 3F 0-6-0T

47307	47500	47521	47606

Class 8F 2-8-0

48077	48427	48550	48688
48203	48493	48554	48757
48207	48534	48610	
48360	48544	48626	
48408	48549	48656	

Class 4 MT 4-6-0

75013	75028	75055

Total 34

4A SHREWSBURY

This depot will be dealt with under 84G (Western Region) as by 1949 this ex-LMS shed was one and the same with the ex-GWR shed which stood alongside (see Introductory Notes).

4B SWANSEA VICTORIA

Pre-Grouping Origin: LNWR
Gazetteer Ref: 43 G3
Closed: 1959
Shed-Codes: 4B (1948-1949)
87K (1949-1959)
Allocations: 1950 (87K)

Class 74xx 0-6-0T

7439

Class 1F 0-6-0T

41769	41824	41852	41860

Class 4MT 2-6-4T

42305	42385	42388	42394
42307	42387	42390	

Class 1P 2-4-2T

46620

Class 3F 0-6-0T

47230	47258	47478	47481
47232	47259	47479	47655
47256	47477	47480	47681

Class 7F 0-8-0

48893	49035	49177	49358
49033	49148	49260	49376

Class 2F 0-6-2T

58892	58910

Class WD 2-8-0

90102	90188	90297	90546	90712
90173	90205	90307	90568	
90186	90225	90359	90579	

Total 48

Allocations: 1959 (87K)

Class PM 0-4-0ST

1152

Class 57xx 0-6-0PT

3694	5761	6700	6714	6749
4676	5773	6702	6720	6753
5728	5793	6712	6738	6763

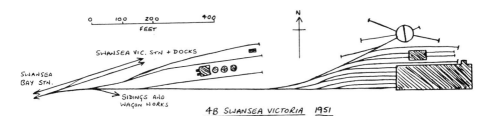

4B SWANSEA VICTORIA 1951

The depot in 1953 (looking east) showing left to right Nos 49035, 7439, an unidentified 57xx and 42307, a typical representation of the period.
Real Photos

6767	6770	6776	6778	8706
6768	6774	6777	6779	

Class 74xx 0-6-0PT
7408

Class 4 2-6-4T

42305	42385	42388	42394
42307	42387	42390	

Class 3F 0-6-0T

47478	47479	47481

Class 8F 2-8-0

48309	48419	48470	48730	48760
48330	48452	48524	48732	48761
48400	48461	48525	48735	48768
48409	48463	48706	48737	

Total 55

4C SWANSEA UPPER BANK

Pre-Grouping Origin: Midland Railway
Gazetteer Ref: 43 G3
Closed: 1963
Shed-Code: 4C (1948-1949)
Allocations: 1954(87K sub)

Class 57xx 0-6-0PT
6720

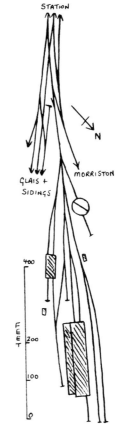

LAYOUT IN 1950

A 1935 view of the depot, looking north-east.
LGRP courtesy David & Charles

Class 1F 0-6-0T
41699	41769	41860

Class 3F 0-6-0T
47230	47256	47478	47480	47681
47232	47258	47479	47655	

Total 13

4D   ABERGAVENNY

Pre-Grouping Origin: LNWR
Gazetteer Ref: 43 A1
Closed: 1958
Shed-Codes: 4D (1948-1949)
86K (1949-1955)
Allocations: 1950(86K)

Class 2MT 2-6-2T
41201	41202	41203	41204

Class 7F 0-8-0
48899	49051	49161	49316
48921	49064	49168	49345
49006	49113	49174	49403
49028	49121	49226	49409
49046	49146	49243	49422

Class 2F 0-6-2T
58880	58895	58912	58916	58933
58888	58899	58913	58919	58935
58891	58902	58915	58925	

Total 38

The shed in 1952 looking south from the road overbridge: on display are a number of Class 2F 0-6-2Ts (otherwise known as 'Webb' Coal Tanks) and Class 7F and 8F freight locos. It will be seen that in this year the covered accommodation had greatly been reduced to six lanes as opposed to the original 12-lane site shown above. Abergavenny was demoted to sub-shed in status by 1955 (becoming sub to 86K). W. Potter

4E TREDEGAR

The shed in 1959, with the station visible on the extreme right (looking north). Photomatic

Pre-Grouping Origin: LNWR
Gazetteer Ref: 43 B1
Closed: 1960
Shed-Codes: 4E (1948-1949)
86K (1955-1960)
Allocations: 1959(86K)

Class 57xx 0-6-0PT
   3700   7721
Class 64xx 0-6-0PT
   6439
Class 3 2-6-2T
   40098   40161   40171
Class 2 2-6-2T
   41201   41204
Class 7F 0-8-0
   49064   49409

Total 10

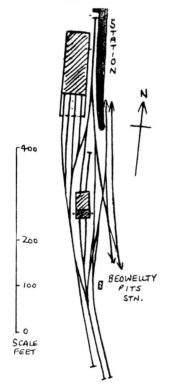

5A CREWE NORTH

Pre-Grouping Origin: LNWR
Gazetteer Ref: 20 E2
Closed: 1965
Shed-Code: 5A (1948-1965)
Allocations: 1950

Class 2P 4-4-0
   40332   40425   40659
   40402   40527   40660
Class 4P 4-4-0
   41112   41115   41160   41167
Class 2MT 2-6-2T
   41229
Class 4MT 2-6-4T
   42308   42677
Class 5MT 4-6-0
   44678   44682   44758   44764   44771
   44679   44683   44761   44765   45217
   44680   44684   44762   44766
   44681   44685   44763   44770
'Patriot' 4-6-0
   45502 *Royal Naval Division*
   45503 *The Leicestershire Regiment*

23

'Patriot' 4-6-0 continued
45504 Royal Signals
45506 The Royal Pioneer Corps
45507 Royal Tank Corps
45510
45511 Isle of Man
45513
45523 Bangor
45528
45529 Stephenson
45535 Sir Herbert Walker KCB
45543 Home Guard
45546 Fleetwood
45548 Lytham St Annes
'Jubilee' 4-6-0
45558 Manitoba
45586 Mysore
45592 Indore
45606 Falkland Islands
45634 Trinidad
45647 Sturdee
45666 Cornwallis
45674 Duncan
45678 De Robeck
45684 Jutland
45686 St Vincent
45689 Ajax
45738 Samson
'Royal Scot' 4-6-0
46113 Cameronian
46128 The Lovat Scouts
46130 The West Yorks Regiment
46146 The Rifle Brigade

46155 The Lancer
46157 The Royal Artilleryman
'Princess' 4-6-2
46204 Princess Louise
46206 Princess Marie Louise
46207 Princess Arthur of Connaught
46208 Princess Helena Victoria
46209 Princess Beatrice
46210 Lady Patricia
46211 Queen Maud
46212 Duchess of Kent
'Coronation' 4-6-2
46233 Duchess of Sutherland
46234 Duchess of Abercorn

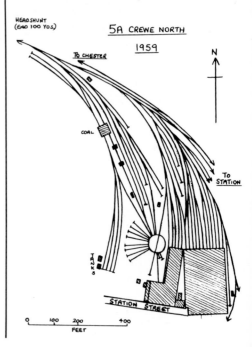

Unrebuilt 'Patriot' Nos 45503 The Royal
Leicestershire Regiment stands between the
turntable and the shed in 1955, facing north. The
shed was situated north-west of platform one of the
station. The footbridge which gave access from this
platform tempted many a spotter to risk the
trespass! An interesting feature of the allocation
totals is the very high number of engines in 1959 by
comparison with the 1950 and obviously less
dieselised period.   B. Morrison

46235 *City of Birmingham*
46236 *City of Bradford*
46243 *City of Lancaster*
46246 *City of Manchester*
46248 *City of Leeds*
Class 2MT 2-6-0
 46457   46458
Class 1P 2-4-2T
 46680
Class 2F 0-6-0
 58388   58429

Total 85

Allocations: 1959

Class 2P 4-4-0
 40652   40655   40660
 40653   40659   40679
Class 2 2-6-2T
 41212   41220   41229
Class 4 2-6-4T
 42575   42578   42677
Class 6P5F 2-6-0
 42946   42955   42961   42966
 42954   42958   42963   42968
Class 5 4-6-0

44678	44759	45021	45243	45369
44679	44760	45033	45250	45373
44680	44761	45073	45254	45379
44682	44762	45093	45257	45390
44683	44763	45113	45282	45434
44684	44764	45148	45289	45446
44685	44765	45189	45305	
44714	44766	45235	45311	
44758	45004	45240	45348	

'Patriot' 4-6-0
 45501 *St Dunstan's*
 45503 *The Royal Leicestershire Regiment*
 45528
 45529 *Stephenson*
 45545 *Planet*
 45546 *Fleetwood*
 45548 *Lytham St Annes*
'Jubilee' 4-6-0
 45553 *Canada*
 45556 *Nova Scotia*
 45591 *Udaipur*
 45604 *Ceylon*
 45623 *Palestine*
 45625 *Sarawak*
 45629 *Straits Settlements*
 45630 *Swaziland*
 45634 *Trinidad*
 45643 *Rodney*
 45655 *Keith*
 45666 *Cornwallis*
 45674 *Duncan*
 45684 *Jutland*
 45689 *Ajax*
 45703 *Thunderer*
 45721 *Impregnable*
 45726 *Vindictive*
 45736 *Phoenix*
'Royal Scot' 4-6-0
 46101 *Royal Scots Grey*
 46110 *Grenadier Guardsman*
 46116 *Irish Guardsman*

46118 *Royal Welch Fusilier*
46120 *Royal Inniskilling Fusiliers*
46125 *3rd Carabinier*
46128 *The Lovat Scouts*
46129 *The Scottish Horse*
46134 *The Cheshire Regiment*
46135 *The East Lancashire Regiment*
46138 *The London Irish Rifleman*
46150 *The Life Guardsman*
46151 *The Royal Horse Guardsman*
46152 *The Kings Dragoon Guardsman*
46157 *The Royal Artilleryman*
46159 *The Royal Air Force*
46163 *Civil Service Rifleman*
'Princess' 4-6-2
46205 *Princess Victoria*
46206 *Princess Marie Louise*
46212 *Duchess of Kent*
'Coronation' 4-6-2
46220 *Coronation*
46221 *Queen Elizabeth*
46225 *Duchess of Gloucester*
46228 *Duchess of Rutland*
46233 *Duchess of Sutherland*
46234 *Duchess of Abercorn*
46235 *City of Birmingham*
46241 *City of Edinburgh*
46243 *City of Lancaster*
46246 *City of Manchester*
46248 *City of Leeds*
46249 *City of Sheffield*
46251 *City of Nottingham*
46252 *City of Leicester*
46253 *City of St Albans*
Class 8P 4-6-2
71000 *Duke of Gloucester*
Class 2 2-6-0
78030

Total 125

Allocations: 1965

Class 2MT 2-6-2T
 41212   41229
Class 5MT 4-6-0

44678	44680	44683	44765
44679	44681	44685	45243

'Britannia' 4-6-2
70000 *Britannia*
70004 *William Shakespeare*
70010 *Owen Glendower*
70012 *John of Gaunt*
70014 *Iron Duke*
70015 *Apollo*
70017 *Arrow*
70018 *Flying Dutchman*
70019 *Lightning*
70020 *Mercury*
70021 *Morning Star*
70023 *Venus*
70024 *Vulcan*
70025 *Western Star*
70027 *Rising Star*
70028 *Royal Star*
70030 *William Wordsworth*
70031 *Byron*
70033 *Charles Dickens*

25

'Britannia' 4-6-2 continued
  70034 *Thomas Hardy*
  70042 *Lord Roberts*
  70043 *Lord Kitchener*
  70044 *Earl Haig*
  70046 *Anzac*
  70050 *Firth of Clyde*
  70051 *Firth of Forth*
  70052 *Firth of Tay*
  70054 *Dornoch Firth*

Total 38

5B   CREWE SOUTH

Pre-Grouping Origin: LNWR
Gazetteer Ref: 20 E2
Closed: 1967
Shed-Code: 5B (1948-1967)
Allocations: 1950

Class 5MT 2-6-0

| 42773 | 42810 | 42815 | 42920 | 42939 |
| 42785 | 42811 | 42856 | 42926 | |

Class 5MT 2-6-0

| 42950 | 42955 | 42968 | 42980 | 42984 |
| 42952 | 42956 | 42972 | 42983 | |

Class 3F 0-6-0

| 43189 | 43207 | | | |

Class 4F 0-6-0

| 44126 | 44300 | 44301 | 44386 | 44452 |

Class 5MT 4-6-0

45006	45060	45134	45239	45300
45013	45067	45148	45240	45301
45030	45073	45185	45254	45369
45038	45093	45189	45270	
45044	45108	45195	45271	
45048	45131	45198	45294	

Class 3F 0-6-0T

47266	47384	47523	47595	47670
47280	47414	47524	47633	47680
47330	47431	47526	47661	
47344	47450	47590	47662	

Class 8F 2-8-0

48248	48256	48287	48296
48249	48257	48288	48297
48250	48259	48289	48757
48251	48260	48290	
48252	48261	48291	
48253	48262	48292	
48254	48263	48294	
48255	48286	48295	

Class 7F 0-8-0

| 49210 | 49230 | 49319 | 49407 |

Class OF 0-4-0ST

| 51204 | 51221 | | |

Total 103

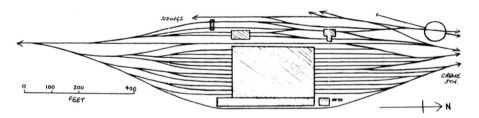

This southern view of the shed in its final year of steam working shows the reduced covered space by this time.   N. E. Preedy

Class 6P5F 2-6-0

42776	42787	42926	42937
42777	42811	42933	42939
42785	42815	42935	

Class 6P5F 2-6-0

42948	42952	42959	42972	42984
42949	42953	42962	42980	
42950	42956	42964	42983	

Class 3F 0-6-0

43464

Class 4F 0-6-0

44186	44344	44385	44595
44301	44359	44592	

Class 5 4-6-0

44681	45000	45060	45134	45299
44713	45002	45067	45142	45300
44832	45003	45074	45149	45301
44834	45044	45108	45188	45391
44868	45045	45128	45198	45403
44871	45048	45131	45270	

Class 3F 0-6-0T

47280	47450	47524	47661
47330	47467	47526	47664
47384	47516	47608	47670
47414	47523	47618	47680

Class 8F 2-8-0

48111	48256	48291	48548	48692
48174	48257	48292	48626	48693
48248	48262	48294	48630	48734
48251	48263	48411	48633	48736
48252	48287	48516	48655	48743
48255	48289	48529	48659	

Class 7F 0-8-0

48922	49158	49407	49454
49048	49229	49417	

Class 3F 0-6-0

52207	52345

Class 2F 0-6-0

58135	58271

Total 117

Stafford was once a two-building site (one six-road, the other four) but it was rebuilt in LMS days to the dimensions shown in the diagram. This 1962 photograph of the rebuilt shed shows (left to right) Stanier Mogul No 42976, a 2-6-4T and a 'Black Five' 4-6-0 outside the six-road structure. W. T. Stubbs

Class 4MT 2-6-0

43001	43024	43034	43088	43151
43020	43026	43052	43113	

Class 5MT 4-6-0

44684	44834	45046	45248	45434
44759	45002	45056	45297	45446
44761	45021	45093	45321	45494
44832	45033	45128	45391	

Class 3F 0-6-0T

47325	47397	47450	47530	47680
47338	47399	47482	47565	
47391	47445	47494	47677	

Class 8F 2-8-0

48035	48255	48398	48551	48736
48251	48292	48502	48630	48743
48252	48305	48505	48633	

Class 2MT 2-6-0

78010	78030	78031	78036

Total 59

5C STAFFORD

Pre-Grouping Origin: LNWR
Gazetteer Ref: 20 G1
Closed: 1965
Shed-Code: 5C (1948-1965)
Allocations: 1950

Class 2P 4-4-0

40322	40443	40471
40405	40461	40507

Class 4MT 2-6-4T

42320	42345	42346	42347	42391

Class 3F 0-6-0T

47588	47606	47653
47598	47649	47665

Class 7F 0-8-0

48922	49115	49229
49047	49158	49410

Total 23

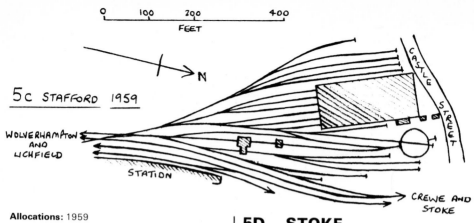

5c STAFFORD **1959**

WOLVERHAMPTON
AND
LICHFIELD

STATION

CREWE AND STOKE

FEET
0   100   200   400

N

Allocations: 1959

Class 2P 4-4-0
  40583   40646   40678
Class 4 2-6-4T
  42309   42389   42425
  42347   42400   42562
Class 3F 0-6-0T
  47359   47588   47649   47665
  47475   47590   47653
Class 7F 0-8-0
  48943   49115   49198   49410
  49081   49126   49357   49446

                      Total 24

Allocations: 1965

Class 4MT 2-6-4T
  42381
Class 5MT 4-6-0
  44813   44963   45110   45147   45374
Class 3F 0-6-0T
  47359   47665
Class 8F 2-8-0
  48602

                      Total 9

5D   STOKE

Pre-Grouping Origin: North Staffordshire Railway
Gazetteer Ref: 20 F1
Closed: 1967
Shed-Code: 5D (1948-1967)
Allocations: 1950

Class 3MT 2-6-2T
  40088   40122   40126   40128   40157
Class 4MT 2-6-4T
  42233   42323   42364   42440   42458
  42234   42343   42375   42443   42479
  42235   42344   42376   42445   42494
  42236   42349   42431   42449   42543

The roundhouse and straight sheds were on opposite sides of the running lines. In 1937 work began on rebuilding the straight shed from nine lanes to eight. A view of the depot in 1939 looking south-east from the coaling tower, with rebuilding still in progress.
A. G. Ellis

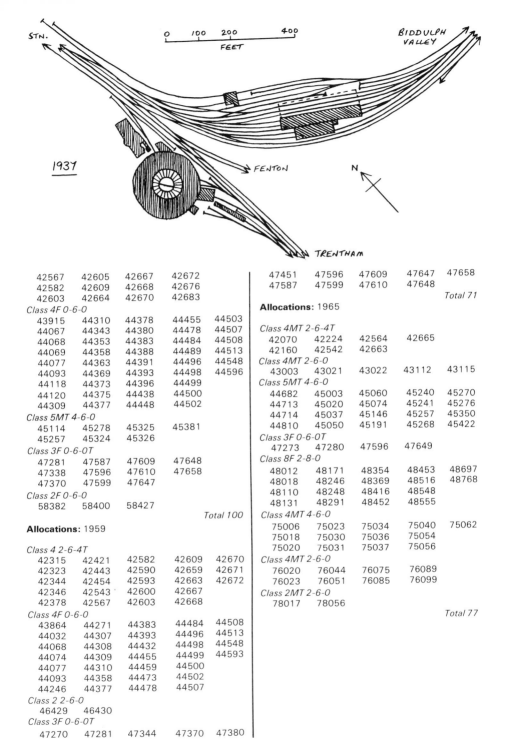

```
42567   42605   42667   42672              47451   47596   47609   47647   47658
42582   42609   42668   42676              47587   47599   47610   47648
42603   42664   42670   42683                                            Total 71
Class 4F 0-6-0                            Allocations: 1965
43915   44310   44378   44455   44503
44067   44343   44380   44478   44507     Class 4MT 2-6-4T
44068   44353   44383   44484   44508       42070   42224   42564   42665
44069   44358   44388   44489   44513       42160   42542   42663
44077   44363   44391   44496   44548     Class 4MT 2-6-0
44093   44369   44393   44498   44596       43003   43021   43022   43112   43115
44118   44373   44396   44499             Class 5MT 4-6-0
44120   44375   44438   44500               44682   45003   45060   45240   45270
44309   44377   44448   44502               44713   45020   45074   45241   45276
Class 5MT 4-6-0                              44714   45037   45146   45257   45350
45114   45278   45325   45381               44810   45050   45191   45268   45422
45257   45324   45326                     Class 3F 0-6-0T
Class 3F 0-6-0T                              47273   47280   47596   47649
47281   47587   47609   47648             Class 8F 2-8-0
47338   47596   47610   47658               48012   48171   48354   48453   48697
47370   47599   47647                       48018   48246   48369   48516   48768
Class 2F 0-6-0                               48110   48248   48416   48548
58382   58400   58427                       48131   48291   48452   48555
                            Total 100     Class 4MT 4-6-0
Allocations: 1959                           75006   75023   75034   75040   75062
                                            75018   75030   75036   75054
Class 4 2-6-4T                              75020   75031   75037   75056
42315   42421   42582   42609   42670     Class 4MT 2-6-0
42323   42443   42590   42659   42671       76020   76044   76075   76089
42344   42454   42593   42663   42672       76023   76051   76085   76099
42346   42543   42600   42667             Class 2MT 2-6-0
42378   42567   42603   42668               78017   78056
Class 4F 0-6-0                                                           Total 77
43864   44271   44383   44484   44508
44032   44307   44393   44496   44513
44068   44308   44432   44498   44548
44074   44309   44455   44499   44593
44077   44310   44459   44500
44093   44358   44473   44502
44246   44377   44478   44507
Class 2 2-6-0
46429   46430
Class 3F 0-6-0T
47270   47281   47344   47370   47380
```

29

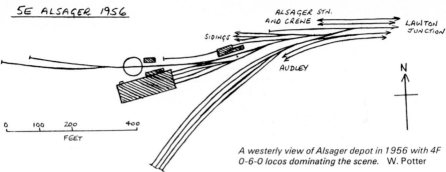

ALSAGER STN.
AND CREWE
LAWTON
JUNCTION
SIDINGS
AUDLEY

N

0   100   200   400
FEET

*A westerly view of Alsager depot in 1956 with 4F
0-6-0 locos dominating the scene.   W. Potter*

5E   ALSAGER

Pre-Grouping Origin: North Staffordshire Railway
Gazetteer Ref: 20 E1
Closed: 1962
Shed-Code: 5E (1948-1962)
Allocations: 1950

Class 4MT 2-6-4T
42309   42447   42471   42611
Class 4F 0-6-0
44063   44125   44342   44359   44453
44079   44341   44344   44450   44595
Class 3F 0-6-0T
47445   47602   47608   47616
                                        Total 18
Allocations: 1959

Class 4F 0-6-0
44063   44125   44354   44450   44503
44067   44342   44386   44452
44079   44352   44405   44453
Class 3F 0-6-0T
47445   47595   47598   47606   47633
                                        Total 18

0   100   200   400
FEET

SIDINGS

5F   UTTOXETER

Pre-Grouping Origin: North Staffordshire Railway
Gazetteer Ref: 15 D5
Closed: 1964
Shed-Code: 5F (1948-1964)
Allocations: 1950

Class 3MT 2-6-2T
40086
Class 4MT 2-6-4T
42358   42663   42665
Class 4F 0-6-0
44307   44504

                            Total 6

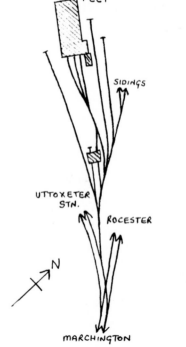

UTTOXETER
STN.

ROCESTER

N

MARCHINGTON

The shed in 1962 with a 'Crab' and two Class 4 tanks on display. The depot was always in the shadow of Stoke (5D) and virtually a sub-shed by comparison. L. Hanson

Allocations: 1959

Class 4 2-6-4T
| 42358 | 42375 | 42605 | 42665 |

Class 4F 0-6-0
| 43877 | 44357 | 44504 |

Total 7

6A CHESTER

Pre-Grouping Origin: LNWR
Gazetteer Ref: 20 D4
Closed: 1967
Shed-Code: 6A (1948-1967)
Allocations: 1950

Class 3MT 2-6-2T
40144

Class 2P 4-4-0
| 40430 | 40658 |

Class 4P 4-4-0
41098	41108	41153	41163	41170
41106	41120	41157	41164	
41107	41121	41158	41169	

Class 4MT 2-6-4T
| 42425 | 42451 | 42540 | 42584 | 42595 |
| 42450 | 42455 | 42568 | 42587 | |

Class 5MT 4-6-0
| 44840 | 45045 | 45247 |
| 44844 | 45095 | 45385 |

Class 3F 0-6-0T
| 47297 | 47375 | 47389 | 47600 |
| 47374 | 47383 | 47504 | |

Total 38

Allocations: 1959

Class 2P 4-4-0
40658

Class 4P 4-4-0
41158

Class 4 2-6-4T
| 42431 | 42544 |

An easterly view in 1961 with various LMS and BR classes on display together with a GWR 'Hall' on the right. An interesting feature of the 1959 allocation was that from a total of only 46 locos no fewer than 10 different classes were represented. W. Potter

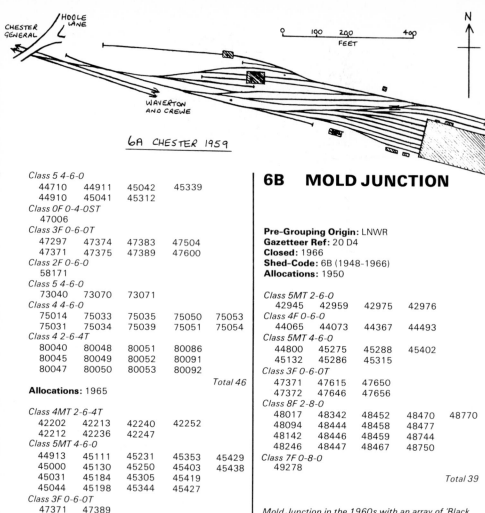

6A CHESTER 1959

Class 5 4-6-0
44710	44911	45042	45339
44910	45041	45312	

Class 0F 0-4-0ST
47006

Class 3F 0-6-0T
47297	47374	47383	47504
47371	47375	47389	47600

Class 2F 0-6-0
58171

Class 5 4-6-0
73040	73070	73071

Class 4 4-6-0
75014	75033	75035	75050	75053
75031	75034	75039	75051	75054

Class 4 2-6-4T
80040	80048	80051	80086
80045	80049	80052	80091
80047	80050	80053	80092

Total 46

Allocations: 1965

Class 4MT 2-6-4T
42202	42213	42240	42252
42212	42236	42247	

Class 5MT 4-6-0
44913	45111	45231	45353	45429
45000	45130	45250	45403	45438
45031	45184	45305	45419	
45044	45198	45344	45427	

Class 3F 0-6-0T
47371	47389

Class 4MT 4-6-0
75010	75012

Total 29

6B   MOLD JUNCTION

Pre-Grouping Origin: LNWR
Gazetteer Ref: 20 D4
Closed: 1966
Shed-Code: 6B (1948-1966)
Allocations: 1950

Class 5MT 2-6-0
42945	42959	42975	42976

Class 4F 0-6-0
44065	44073	44367	44493

Class 5MT 4-6-0
44800	45275	45288	45402
45132	45286	45315	

Class 3F 0-6-0T
47371	47615	47650
47372	47646	47656

Class 8F 2-8-0
48017	48342	48452	48470	48770
48094	48444	48458	48477	
48142	48446	48459	48744	
48246	48447	48467	48750	

Class 7F 0-8-0
49278

Total 39

Mold Junction in the 1960s with an array of 'Black Five' and Class 8Fs. The rear of a Class 9F 2-10-0 can also be seen near the centre of the view. N. Skinner

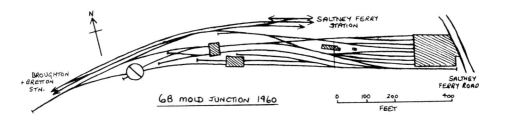

Allocations: 1959

6C BIRKENHEAD

Class 6P5F 2-6-0

42945	42965	42971	42976	42982
42960	42967	42973	42981	

Class 4F 0-6-0

43908	44065	44073	44117	44493

Class 5 4-6-0

44800	45028	45130	45325
44971	45043	45247	45345
45001	45055	45275	

Class 3F 0-6-0T

47615	47646	47650

Class 8F 2-8-0

48246	48259	48458

Class WD 2-8-0

90147	90187	90257	90532	90702
90157	90227	90317	90566	
90178	90242	90423	90606	

Total 44

Allocations: 1965

Class 5MT 4-6-0

44800	44917	45043	45325
44842	44971	45237	45395
44897	45042	45275	

Class 3F 0-6-0T

47350	47673

Class 8F 2-8-0

48090	48259	48632
48094	48269	48655
48173	48287	48667
48175	48411	48723
48253	48458	48749

Total 28

Pre-Grouping Origin: LNW/GWR Joint Railway
Gazetteer Ref: 45 F4
Closed: 1967
Shed-Codes: 6C (1948-1963)
8H (1963-1967)
Allocations: 1950 (6C)

Class 14xx 0-4-2T
1417

Class 1901 0-6-0T

1917	1968	2004

Class 2021 0-6-0T

2067	2092	2106	2129	2156
2089	2104	2108	2152	

Class 57xx 0-6-0T

3626	7714	9651
3742	8725	9678

*Looking towards the LNWR building in 1954
showing Nos 1457 and 2822. Originally, the
buildings were of equal length; however the LNWR
shed was cut-back in size during LMS days. In 1954
a large part of the GWR building had fallen into
disuse thus resulting in the ex-GWR locos regular
appearance on the 'foreign' side. On the right of the
view, can be seen the ex-GWR building (south-west
wall) clearly portraying the northlight roof pattern
favoured by that company. H. C. Casserley*

Class 51xx 2-6-2T
4120	4123	4125	4127	4129
4122	4124	4126	4128	5176

Class 47xx 2-8-0
4704

Class 43xx 2-6-0
5316	5393	6346	6350	6376

'Grange' 4-6-0
6831 Bearley Grange
6841 Marlas Grange
6844 Penydd Grange
6859 Yiewsley Grange
6860 Aberporth Grange
6878 Longford Grange

Class 3MT 2-6-2T
40101	40104	40121	40131	40207
40102	40110	40129	40132	

Class 1F 0-6-0T
41734	41780	41853

Class 5MT 2-6-0
42953	42967	42970
42961	42969	42981

Class 2F 0-6-0T
47160	47164	47166

Class 3F 0-6-0T
47324	47507	47627	47672
47472	47530	47628	47674

Class 8F 2-8-0
48106	48344	48455	48673	48691
48247	48448	48491	48684	

Class 2F 0-6-0ST
51313	51441

Class 3F 0-6-0
52208	52225	52232	52270	52432

Class 2F 0-6-0T
58851	58854	58857	58861	58863

Class WD 2-8-0
90135	90143

Total 93

Allocations: 1959 (6C)

Class 850 0-6-0PT
2012
Class 2021 0-6-0PT
2069
Class 3 2-6-2T
40101	40121	40202
40102	40131	40209

Class 2 2-6-2T
41324
Class 4 2-6-4T
42447	42493	42597	42599	42608

Class 6P5F 2-6-0
42778	42856	42888	42894	42941

Class 6P5F 2-6-0
42969	42970	42977	42978

Class 5 4-6-0
44917
Class 0F 0-4-0ST
47005	47009

Class 2F 0-6-0T
47160	47164

Class 3F 0-6-0T
47324	47431	47507	47565	47674
47338	47497	47530	47627	47677

Class 8F 2-8-0
48120	48349	48455	48691
48260	48448	48684	

Class 5 4-6-0
73032	73039

Class 4 2-6-4T
80062	80063	80090

Class 2 2-6-2T
84000	84003

Class WD 2-8-0
90173	90212	90369	90392

Total 56

Allocations: 1965 (8H)

Class 4MT 2-6-4T
42086	42104	42121	42566	42597

Class 5MT 2-6-0
42753	42782	42827	42936
42765	42783	42859	42937
42777	42814	42924	

Class 3F 0-6-0T
47272	47423	47495	47627	47674
47324	47447	47533	47659	

Class 8F 2-8-0
48062	48323	48435	48448	48716
48257	48348	48441	48668	48771
48260	48373	48446	48684	
48262	48423	48447	48691	

Class 9F 2-10-0
92020	92084	92105	92120	92157
92045	92085	92106	92121	92165
92046	92089	92107	92122	92166
92047	92100	92108	92123	92167
92057	92101	92109	92127	
92079	92102	92111	92133	
92082	92103	92112	92134	

Total 75

The depot's unusual mixture of classes was primarily due to the ex-GWR allocation remaining after the shed became the whole responsibility of the London Midland Region in 1951. This situation existed until 1963 when all the GWR types were re-allocated or withdrawn from service. It will be seen that from the 1959 figures no fewer than 16 different classes were evident amongst a mere total of 56 locomotives!

1954

A southerly view of the diminutive two road depot in 1953. Class 3MT No 40209 is the loco nearest the camera, whilst a Class N5 0-6-2T occupies the right background. Real Photos

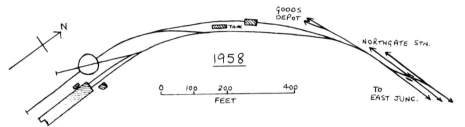

6D CHESTER NORTHGATE

went to the breaker's yard. As the above listings indicate, this metamorphosis was complete by the late 1950s.

Pre-Grouping Origin: Cheshire Lines Railway
Gazetteer Ref: 20 D4
Closed: 1960
Shed-Code: 6D (1949-1960)
Allocations: 1950

Class J10 0-6-0
  65143   65167
Class C13 4-4-2T
  67400   67414   67436
  67413   67433
Class N5 0-6-2T
  69274   69281
                              Total 9

Allocations: 1959

Class 2 2-6-2T
  41214
Class 4 2-6-4T
  42303   42308   42415   42417
Class 2 2-6-0
  78031   78055   78056   78058   78059
Class 2 2-6-2T
  84001
                              Total 11

The all ex-GCR 1950 stud was gradually replaced by LMS and BR stock as the vintage locomotives

6E WREXHAM RHOSDDU

Pre-Grouping Origin: GCR
Gazetteer Ref: 20 E4
Closed: 1960 (Used for locomotive storage until 1964)
Shed-Codes: 6E (1949-1958)
84K (1958-1960)
Allocations: 1950 (6E)

Class 3MT 2-6-2T
  40085   40103   40127   40156
Sentinel 0-4-0T
  47184
Class J11 0-6-0
  64338   64381
Class C13 4-4-2T
  67428   67429   67430   67432   67435
Class C14 4-4-2T
  67442   67449
Class J94 0-6-0ST
  68063
Class Y3 0-4-0T
  68163   68164

35

The shed in 1952 with two Class N5s Nos 69346
and 69352, also Class C13 No 67430 (all of 6E).
The N5s were mainly responsible for the Brymbo
steelworks shunt. LGRP courtesy David & Charles

6E WREXHAM RHOSDDU

1957

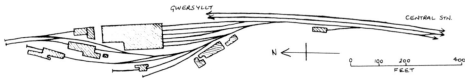

Class J62 0-6-0ST
  68200
Class J67 0-6-0T
  68531
Class N5 0-6-2T

69267	69329	69340	69349	69362
69290	69330	69346	69352	69366

Total 29

Allocations: 1959(84K)
Class 16xx 0-6-0PT

1618	1663	1669

Class 2251 0-6-0

3201	3204	3207

Class 57xx 0-6-0PT

3749	3760	4683	8734	9610

Class 56xx 0-6-2T

5606	5651	6610

Class 3 2-6-2T

40085	40086	40110	40126	40205

Class 2 2-6-2T

41231	41232

Class 3 2-6-2T

82000	82020	82021	82031	82037

Total 26

6F BIDSTON

Pre-Grouping Origin: GCR
Gazetteer Ref: 45 F4
Closed: 1963
Shed-Code: 6F (1949-1963)
Allocations: 1950

Class J94 0-6-0ST

68006	68065	68066

Class J72 0-6-0T

68671	68701	68714	68727

Class N5 0-6-2T
  69289

Total 8

The depot in 1961 looking east with two Class 8F
freight engines simmering alongside the dockland
shed. M. S. Houlgrave

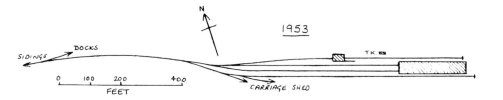

DOCKS
SIDINGS
TK
FEET
CARRIAGE SHED

0   100   200   400

Allocations: 1959

Class 2F 0-6-0T
47166
Class 3F 0-6-0T
47622   47628
Class 8F 2-8-0
48253   48667
Class J94 0-6-0ST
68063   68065   68066
Class J72 0-6-0T
68671   68714   68727
Class 9F 2-10-0
92045   92046   92047

Total 14

The allocation of class 2F 0-6-0T No 47166 in 1959 was evidence of the short radius work that this dockside depot had to undertake. (The J94 class was also of short wheelbase, ideal for dockside use.)

7A LLANDUDNO JUNCTION

Pre-Grouping Origin: LNWR
Gazetteer Ref: 19 D3
Closed: 1966
Shed-Codes: 7A (1948-1952)
6G (1952-1966)
Allocations: 1950(7A)

Class 3MT 2-6-2T
40083   40133
40123   40137
40130   40209

Class 4P 4-4-0
40925   41086   41114   41123   41150
40933   41093   41119   41124   41161
Class 2MT 2-6-2T
41232
Class 4F 0-6-0
43877   44389
Class 5MT 4-6-0
44738   44740   44742   45241
44739   44741   44971   45292
Class 1P 2-4-2T
46604
Class 3F 0-6-0T
47394
Class 2F 0-6-0
58364   58365

Total 31

Allocations: 1959(6G)

Class 3 2-6-2T
40008   40058   40095   40128   40133
40048   40073   40123   40130
Class 2P 4-4-0
40635   40675   40699
Class 4P 4-4-0
41120
Class 2 2-6-2T
41226   41236   41238   41322
41235   41237   41244   41323
Class 4F 0-6-0
44389   44525

A view of the eastern end of the depot in 1935. Although the shed only had a few express locomotives allocated during BR days, it often played host to the visiting 'Scots', 'Jubilees' and 'Patriots' which brought in the majority of the coastal excursions. LGRP courtesy David & Charles

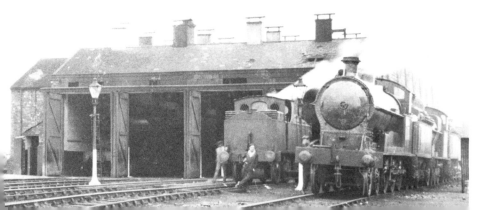

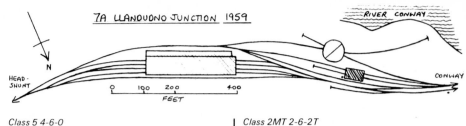

RIVER CONWAY

N

HEAD-SHUNT

CONWAY

FEET
0   100   200   400

Class 5 4-6-0
44738   44740   44865   45180
44739   44864   44935
Class 3F 0-6-0T
47372   47394   47631
Class 4 4-6-0
75010   75011   75012   75013   75032
Total 38

Allocations: 1965(6G)

Class 2MT 2-6-2T
41201   41202   41220   41232   41272
Class 5MT 4-6-0
45004   45116   45277   45285
45045   45143   45279   45311
45091   45149   45282   45348
Class 3F 0-6-0T
47361   47507   47598
Class 2MT 2-6-2T
84003   84009
Total 22

Class 2MT 2-6-2T
41223   41224   41233
Class 4MT 2-6-4T
42156   42259   42460   42628
42157   42260   42588   42660
42258   42261   42617
Class 4F 0-6-0
44305   44445
Class 5MT 4-6-0
44913   45144
Class 2MT 0-6-2T
46899   46906
Class 3F 0-6-0
52119   52176   52230   52269   52407
Class 2F 0-6-0
58375   58381
Class 2F 0-6-2T
58903
Total 32

7B BANGOR

Pre-Grouping Origin: LNWR
Gazetteer Ref: 19 D2
Closed: 1965
Shed-Codes: 7B (1948-1952)
6H (1952-1965)
Allocations: 1950(7B)

Class 3MT 2-6-2T
40124   40134   40143
Class 2P 4-4-0
40524

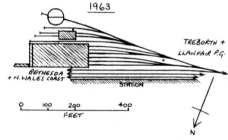

1963

TREBORTH +
LLANFAIR P.G.

BETHESDA
+ N. WALES COAST

STATION

FEET
0   100   200   400

N

The shed and station in 1956 looking east. In the centre is one of Bangor's Class 3F 0-6-0 allocation, No 52230 at the head of goods stock awaiting a clear road. On the left a local passenger train stands at the station with a 2-6-4T in command. The roof was renewed in 1957.   B. Hilton

Allocations: 1959(6H)

Class 3 2-6-2T
40071 40132 40136 40185
Class 2 2-6-2T
41200 41230 41233 41234 41239
Class 4F 0-6-0
44305 44445
Class 5 4-6-0
44913 45144 45417
Class 3F 0-6-0T
47511 47558
Class 2 2-6-0
78057
Class 4 2-6-4T
80087 80088 80089 80094 80095
Total 22

Allocations: 1965(6H)

Class 2MT 2-6-2T
41200 41233 41234
Class 4MT 2-6-4T
42074 42251 42267 42283 42606
Class 5MT 4-6-0
44821 45145 45223 45298 45345
Class 4MT 4-6-0
75035
Class 2MT 2-6-0
78003 78032 78058 78059
Class 4MT 2-6-4T
80131
Class 3MT 2-6-2T
82032
Total 20

Pre-Grouping Origin: LNWR
Gazetteer Ref: 19 B2
Closed: 1966
Shed-Codes: 7C (1948-1952)
6J (1952-1966)
Allocations: 1950(7C)

Class 5MT 4-6-0
44808 45070 45113 45376
44868 45110 45249 45382
45028 45111 45346
'Patriot' 4-6-0
45534 E. Tootal Broadhurst
'Royal Scot' 4-6-0
46112 Sherwood Forester
46119 Lancashire Fusilier
46127 Old Contemptibles
46132 The King's Regiment Liverpool
46158 The Loyal Regiment
46161 King's Own
46165 The Ranger (12th London Regiment)
46166 London Rifle Brigade
Class 3F 0-6-0T
47321 47368 47476
Total 23

Allocations: 1959 (6J)

Class 5 4-6-0
44661 44986 45110 45429
44802 45056 45382 45441

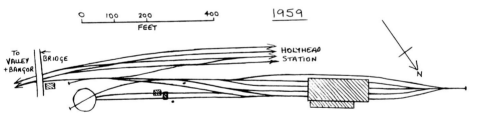

A 1960 view depicting a WD 2-8-0, a 'Royal Scot' 4-6-0 and a 'Jinty' 0-6-0T. The shed's main function was to provide motive power and facilities for the 'Boat Trains' to and from Ireland hence the allocation of express engines.   T. Nicholls

'Royal Scot' 4-6-0
46127 Old Contemptibles
46149 The Middlesex Regiment
Class 3F 0-6-0T

47321	47368	47439	47476

'Britannia' 4-6-2
70045 Lord Rowallan
70046*
70047
70048 The TA 1908-1958
70049*

Total 19

Allocations: 1965(6J)

Class 5MT 4-6-0

44711	44770	45132	45300
44712	44807	45247	

Class 3F 0-6-0T

47266	47321	47410	47439

'Britannia' 4-6-2
70026 Polar Star
70045 Lord Rowallan
70047
70053 Moray Firth

Total 15

*In 1959 No 70046 (*Anzac*) and No 70049 (*Solway Firth*) had not yet received their names.

7D   RHYL

Pre-Grouping Origin: LNWR
Gazetteer Ref: 19 C5
Closed: 1963
Shed-Codes 7D (1948-1952) 6K (1952-1963)
Allocations: 1950 (7D)

Class 2P 4-4-0

40324	40396	40495	40646	40675
40377	40433	40629	40671	

Class 2MT 2-6-2T

41210	41211	41231

Class 3F 0-6-0
43396
Class 2P 2-4-2T

50678	50687

Class 3F 0-6-0

52125	52172	52338	52453
52167	52233	52356	

Class 2F 0-6-0

58392	58420

Class 2F 0-6-2T

58889	58924	58932

Total 27

Allocations: 1959 (6K)

Class 2P 4-4-0
40589
Class 2 2-6-2T

41216	41276

Class 3F 0-6-0

43378	43618

Class 4F 0-6-0

43981	44367

Class 2 2-6-0
46445
Class 3F 0-6-0T
47350
Class 3F 0-6-0

52119	52162

Class 2F 0-6-0
58287, 58293
Class 2 2-6-0
78038

Total 14

Of the nine classes of locomotive represented in 1959, it will be noted that only 14 engines were allocated in all, thus creating a highly mixed bag of motive power. Also interesting to note is the fact that by this time the only surviving pre-Grouping engines were ex-Midland and ex-L&Y stock despite the depot's LNWR roots.

This 1952 view depicts from left to right No 40580 (6K), 42663 and 41120 (6A). The latter engine having worked in with a special excursion. The conversation of the two men could well be about No 41120's failure to comply with a well portrayed depot regulation! Real Photos

A 1960 view of Liverpool's main depot Edge Hill, one of the Late Bishop Treacy's most popular subjects. The shed was quite a size despite it being situated amongst a maze of goods and passenger lines, not all of which are shown in the diagram for space reasons. Towards the end of its existence as a steam depot six of the south-west dead-end roads were uprooted in favour of a two road diesel servicing structure. The roof pattern was of the usual LMS style (see 6C), until closure. P. H. Hanson

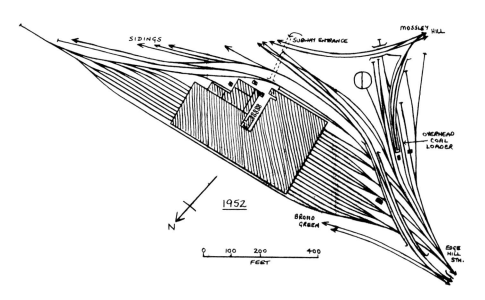

SIDINGS

SUBWAY ENTRANCE

MOSSLEY HILL

OVERHEAD COAL LOADER

1952

N

BROAD GREEN

EDGE HILL STN.

0   100   200   400
FEET

8A   EDGE HILL

Pre-Grouping Origin: LNWR
Gazetteer Ref: 45 F4
Closed: 1968
Shed-Code: 8A (1948-1968)
Allocations: 1950

Class 3MT 2-6-2T
40001   40003   40007
Class 4MT 2-6-4T
42426   42459   42564   42570   42583

| 42596 | 42597 | 42602 | 42612 | 42658 |

Class 5MT 4-6-0

44768	45005	45256	45380
44769	45017	45276	45393
44772	45181	45303	45398
44906	45242	45347	45399
44907	45243	45350	
44941	45248	45352	

'Patriot' 4-6-0
45515 Caernarvon
45527 Southport
45531 Sir Frederick Harrison
45533 Lord Rathmore
45538 Giggleswick

41

'Jubilee' 4-6-0
45567 South Australia
45613 Kenya
45623 Palestine
45637 Windward Islands
45670 Howard of Effingham
45673 Keppel
45681 Aboukir
45721 Impregnable
45737 Atlas
'Royal Scot' 4-6-0
46106 Gordon Highlander
46111 Royal Fusilier
46123 Royal Irish Fusilier
46124 London Scottish
46125 3rd Carabinier
46134 The Cheshire Regiment
46135 The East Lancashire Regiment
46137 The Prince of Wales Volunteers
(South Lancashire)
46138 The London Irish Rifleman
46144 Honourable Artillery Company
46153 The Royal Dragoon
46156 The South Wales Borderer
46164 The Artists' Rifleman
'Princess Royal' 4-6-2
46200 The Princess Royal
46201 Princess Elizabeth
46203 Princess Margaret Rose
46205 Princess Victoria
Class 3F 0-6-0T

47294	47325	47385	47404	47597
47309	47353	47392	47407	
47320	47357	47402	47416	

Class 7F 0-8-4T

47931	47937	47939

Class 8F 2-8-0

48457	48510	48512	48513

Class 7F 0-8-0

48898	49126	49301	49412	49449
48932	49137	49355	49419	
48933	49224	49399	49437	
48943	49239	49404	49445	

Class 2F 0-6-0ST

51353	51445

Class 3F 0-6-0

52111	52118	52321	52330

Class 2F 0-6-2T

58887	58911	58921

Total 112

Allocations: 1959

Class 4 2-6-4T

42121	42441	42564	42583
42155	42459	42570	42602

Class 5 4-6-0

44768	44907	45181	45343	45401
44769	45005	45242	45376	45410
44772	45032	45249	45380	45413
44773	45039	45256	45398	45421
44906	45069	45276	45399	

'Patriot' 4-6-0
45515 Caernarvon
45516 The Beds & Herts Regiment
45518 Bradshaw
45521 Rhyl

45525 Colwyn Bay
45527 Southport
45531 Sir Frederick Harrison
45534 E. Tootal Broadhurst
45535 Sir Herbert Walker KCB
45539 E. C. Trench

45544	45549	45550

'Jubilee' 4-6-0
45552 Silver Jubilee
45554 Ontario
45560 Prince Edward Island
45567 South Australia
45583 Assam
45586 Mysore
45596 Bahamas
45670 Howard of Effingham
45678 De Robeck
45681 Aboukir
45733 Novelty
'Royal Scot' 4-6-0
46114 Coldstream Guardsman
46119 Lancashire Fusilier
46123 Royal Irish Fusilier
46124 London Scottish
46132 The King's Regiment Liverpool
46142 The York and Lancaster Regiment
46147 The Northamptonshire Regiment
46155 The Lancer
46156 The South Wales Borderer
46164 The Artists' Rifleman
'Princess Royal' 4-6-2
46200 The Princess Royal
46203 Princess Margaret Rose
46204 Princess Louise
46207 Princess Arthur of Connaught
46208 Princess Helena Victoria
46209 Princess Beatrice
46211 Queen Maud
Class 3F 0-6-0T

47353	47404	47416	47489	47566
47357	47407	47487	47498	47597
47402	47411	47488	47519	47656

Class 8F 2-8-0

48152	48318	48479	48512
48249	48433	48504	48513
48280	48457	48509	

Class 7F 0-8-0

49082	49200	49392	49412	49434
49116	49224	49394	49416	49435
49132	49355	49399	49419	49437
49137	49366	49404	49427	49445
49173	49375	49405	49429	

Class 2F 0-6-0ST

51445

Total 124

Allocations: 1965

Class 5MT 4-6-0

44768	44907	45187	45307
44769	44964	45242	45312
44772	45005	45249	45376
44773	45015	45261	45402
44827	45039	45284	45440
44838	45069		
44864	45094		
44906	45156 Ayrshire Yeomanry		

42

Class 3F 0-6-0T
47285   47406   47416   47519
47357   47415   47487
Class 8F 2-8-0
48029   48152   48249   48433   48746
48078   48163   48280   48512
48129   48188   48296   48513
48151   48200   48308   48742
Total 50

8B WARRINGTON DALLAM

Pre-Grouping Origin: LNWR
Gazetteer Ref: 45 D4
Closed: 1967
Shed-Code: 8B (1948-1967)
Allocations: 1950

Class 3MT 2-6-2T
40042
Class 4MT 2-6-4T
42606   42607
Class 3F 0-6-0
43237   43283   43329   43398   43618
43282   43314   43389   43615   43657

Class 5MT 4-6-0
44897   45035   45149   45255   45328
45001   45072   45196   45305   45354
45032   45109   45252   45321   45370
'Patriot' 4-6-0
45521 Rhyl
Class 1P 2-4-2T
46603   46654   46688   46701
Class 3F 0-6-0T
47268   47376   47591   47652   47657
47352   47387   47603   47654
Class 8F 2-8-0
48366   48466   48473   48689
48436   48469   48664
Class 7F 0-8-0
49008,   49119   49149   49247
Class 2P 2-4-2T
50697   50703   50705
Class 3F 0-6-0
52088   52598   52608
Total 59

Allocations: 1959

Class 3 2-6-2T
40125   40156
Class 2 2-6-2T
41210   41213
Class 4 2-6-4T
42606   42607
Class 3F 0-6-0
43237   43308   43387   43615   43651
43282   43314   43398   43619   43657

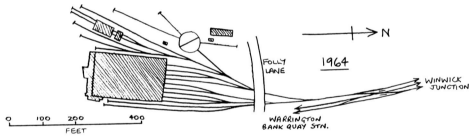

A southerly view of Dallam in 1955 with Stanier Class 5 and 8F locos dominating the scene. The depot began acquiring some 'Jubilees' in 1961.
W. Potter

Class 4F 0-6-0
| 44237 | 44356 | 44384 |

Class 5 4-6-0
| 45035 | 45252 | 45271 | 45328 | 45495 |
| 45196 | 45255 | 45321 | 45354 | |

Class 3F 0-6-0T
47268	47376	47603	47657
47352	47387	47652	47659
47362	47591	47654	

Class 8F 2-8-0
48094	48247	48373	48531	48715
48106	48296	48441	45683	48746
48188	48348	48520	48714	

Total 53

Allocations: 1965

Class 4F 0-6-0
| 44115 | 44181 | 44294 | 44349 | 44522 |

Class 5MT 4-6-0
44658	44819	45041	45129	45303
44730	44930	45078	45238	45436
44731	44935	45109	45256	

'Jubilee' 4-6-0
| 45563 Australia |
| 45590 Travancore |
| 45633 Aden |

Class 9F 2-10-0
92048	92058	92086	92126
92049	92059	92116	92156
92053	92070	92119	92160
92055	92078	92124	92163

Total 38

8C SPEKE JUNCTION

Pre-Grouping Origin: LNWR
Gazetteer Ref: 45 E4
Closed: 1968
Shed-Code: 8C (1948-1968)
Allocations: 1950

Class 5MT 2-6-0
| 42849 | 42852 | 42892 |

Class 5MT 2-6-0
| 42962 | 42965 | 42977 |
| 42964 | 42971 | 42982 |

Class 3F 0-6-0T
| 47284 | 47373 | 47439 |
| 47362 | 47388 | 47651 |

Class 8F 2-8-0
| 48520 | 48522 | 48529 | 48631 | 48747 |
| 48521 | 48528 | 48630 | 48743 | 48748 |

Class 7F 0-8-0
48942	49120	49212	49249	49395
48944	49125	49218	49253	49420
49074	49143	49219	49293	
49105	49172	49244	49302	

Class 2F 0-6-0ST
| 51439 |

Class 3F 0-6-0
| 52100 | 52143 | 52163 | 52175 | 52438 |

Total 49

Allocations: 1959

Class 6P5F 2-6-0
| 42849 | 42892 |

Class 3F 0-6-0T
| 47314 | 47493 | 47612 |
| 47388 | 47560 | 47651 |

Class 8F 2-8-0
| 48039 | 48206 | 48323 | 48522 | 48747 |
| 48054 | 48264 | 48511 | 48631 | |

Class 7F 0-8-0
48942	49134	49306	49406	49433
48944	49143	49397	49420	49451
49008	49153	49398	49424	

Class 3F 0-6-0
| 52232 | 52438 |

Total 33

The depot in 1966 looking east. The threat of complete dieselisation is shown here as they occupy four of the 12 roads. The role of the depot was mainly to supply south Liverpool's freight and shunting needs. W. Potter

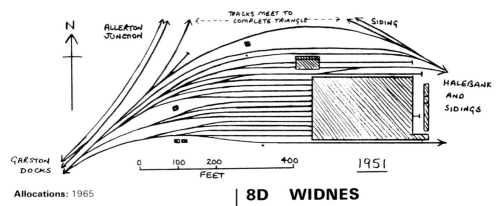

Allocations: 1965

8D WIDNES

Class 5MT 4-6-0

44725	45034	45181	45332	45407
44732	45057	45188	45338	45412
44743	45059	45201	45370	45417
44753	45071	45212	45386	45441
44806	45131	45329	45388	45466
44877	45137			
44950	45154 *Lanarkshire Yeomanry*			

Class 2MT 2-6-0

46410	46440	46515	46518
46424	46503	46516	

Class 8F 2-8-0

48189	48457	48520	48711
48294	48476	48692	48722
48425	48509	48709	48774

Class 9F 2-10-0

92008	92027	92104	92117	92158
92025	92054	92115	92131	

Total 57

Pre-Grouping Origin: LNWR
Gazetteer Ref: 45 D4
Closed: 1964
Shed-Code: 8D (1948-1964)
Allocations: 1950

Class 3P 2-6-2T
40125

Class 2MT 2-6-0

46420	46421	46422	46423	46424

Class 8F 2-8-0

48462	48558	48753	48771
48554	48708	48764	48772

Class 7F 0-8-0

49020	49073	49079	49116	49343

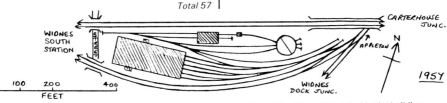

Looking towards the shed from the east in 1961. On view are 2-6-0 No 78035, and 2-6-2T No 41244 together with a Class 8F just inside the building.
W. T. Stubbs

45

Class 2F 0-6-0
| 58363 | 58383 | 58413 | 58430 |
| 58373 | 58393 | 58415 | |

Class J67 0-6-0T
68547

Total 27

Allocations: 1959

Class 3 2-6-2T
| 40134 | 40137 | 40143 | 40201 |

Class 3F 0-6-0T
| 47490 | 47616 |

Class 8F 2-8-0
48166	48326	48506	48697	48753
48175	48425	48554	48709	48771
48308	48502	48558	48749	

Class OF 0-4-0ST
51218

Class J10 0-6-0
| 65184 | 65198 |

Class 2 2-6-0
| 78032 | 78033 | 78034 | 78035 | 78039 |

Total 28

The allocation of those locomotives prefixed with a 6 was a product of the Cheshire Lines Railway's association with the area and nationalisation will have put the ex-GER and GCR engines under the London Midland Region's control.

8E BRUNSWICK

Pre-Grouping Origin: Cheshire Lines Railway
Gazetteer Ref: 45 F4
Closed: 1961
Shed-Codes: 13E (1949)
8E (1949-1958)
27F (1958-1961)
Allocations: 1950 (8E)

Class 3MT 2-6-2T
40180

Class 2P 4-4-0
| 40397 | 40522 | 40583 | 40683 |
| 40464 | 40529 | 40679 | |

Class 4P 4-4-0
| 40926 | 41156 | 41166 |
| 41118 | 41162 | 41173 |

Class 5MT 2-6-0
42949

Class J11 0-6-0
| 64304 | 64405 | 64417 |
| 64376 | 64406 | 64420 |

Class J10 0-6-0
| 65126 | 65142 | 65153 | 65163 | 65182 |
| 65136 | 65149 | 65155 | 65172 | |

Class J69 0-6-0T
68559

Class N5 0-6-2T
| 69254 | 69272 | 69339 |
| 69258 | 69288 | 69342 |

Total 37

Allocations: 1959 (27F)

Class 3 2-6-2T
| 40127 | 40203 |

Brunswick MPD, south Liverpool was slightly curved in shape to give maximum covered accommodation from the cramped space allowed. By 1950, 90ft or so of the roofing had disappeared as will be seen in the photograph. Looking north-west into the shed in 1950 a Class D11 (ex-GCR 'Director') can be seen silhouetted at the entrance. Although its number cannot be read, it can be safely assumed that it is one of the following Nos 62663 Prince Albert, 62665 Mons or 62670 Marne. These were the only three allocated to the LM Region from a class of 35 in this year. On the right hand side Class N5 0-6-2T No 69272 can be seen also. Most of the ex-Cheshire Lines depots had an allocation of these engines at one time or another and No 69272 was one of six allocated to Brunswick at this time.   H. C. Casserley

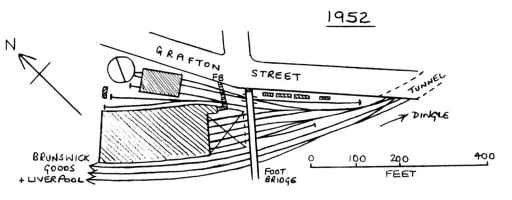

Class 4 2-6-4T				
42146	42352	42580	42598	
42183	42445	42584	42612	
42349	42448	42596		

Class 4F 0-6-0

43910	44154	44396	44587	
43915	44232	44489	44589	
44127	44293	44494		

Class 5 4-6-0

45217	45262	45346	45444	

Class 3F 0-6-0T

47320	47325	47327	47367	47611

Total 33

Class 3MT 2-6-2T

40077	40107	40136

Class 2P 4-4-0

40539	40674	40693

Class 4P 4-4-0

41113	41159	41168

Class 2P 0-4-4T

41905	41906	41907

Class 4MT 2-6-4T

42322	42398	42461	42575	42608
42350	42399	42467	42580	
42351	42427	42478	42594	
42397	42430	42542	42599	

9A LONGSIGHT

Pre-Grouping Origin: LNWR
Gazetteer Ref: 45 A3
Closed: 1965
Shed-Code: 9A (1948-1965)
Allocations: 1950

This 1960 view of the south shed shows two 'Crab' 2-6-0s, Nos 42854 (9B) and 42923 (9A). Between them is a Class 7F 0-8-0, No 49210, a Buxton engine. The south shed was modernised in 1957 to service diesels as well as steam and the result was a smaller six road building which, as can be seen, hinted at the prospect of early dieselisation for the depot. The north shed was mainly the haunt of the passenger locos, both allocated and visiting.
Photomatic

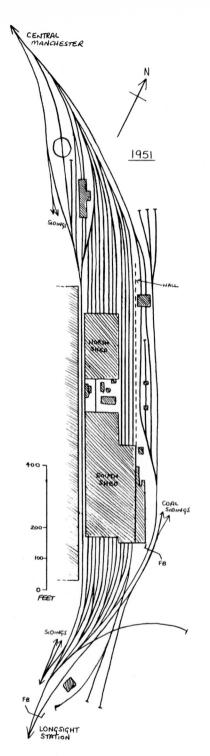

Class 5MT 2-6-0

42772	42788	42886	42924	42936
42775	42848	42887	42925	42937
42776	42854	42889	42930	42938
42778	42858	42923	42935	

Class 5MT 2-6-0

42978	42979

Class 3F 0-6-0

43275	43457	43717

Class 4F 0-6-0

44271	44303	44308	44349	44357

Class 5MT 4-6-0

44748	44752	44832	44935	45387
44749	44759	44834	44937	
44750	44760	44837	45289	
44751	44807	44838	45307	

'Patriot' 4-6-0
45500 *Patriot*
45501 *St Dunstan's*
45520 *Llandudno*
45530 *Sir Frank Ree*
45536 *Private W. Wood VC*
45539 *E. C. Trench*
45540 *Sir Robert Turnbull*

'Jubilee' 4-6-0
45556 *Nova Scotia*
45593 *Kolhapur*
45603 *Solomon Islands*
45617 *Mauritius*
45631 *Tanganyika*
45632 *Tonga*
45633 *Aden*
45638 *Zanzibar*
45655 *Keith*
45680 *Camperdown*
45688 *Polyphemus*
45709 *Implacable*
45723 *Fearless*
45734 *Meteor*
45740 *Munster*

'Royal Scot' 4-6-0
46114 *Coldstream Guardsman*
46115 *Scots Guardsman*
46120 *Royal Inniskilling Fusilier*
46122 *Royal Ulster Rifleman*
46129 *The Scottish Horse*
46131 *The Royal Warwickshire Regiment*
46143 *The South Staffordshire Regiment*
46145 *The Duke of Wellington's Regiment*
       (W. Riding)
46149 *The Middlesex Regiment*
46150 *The Life Guardsman*
46160 *Queen Victoria's Rifleman*
46167 *The Herts Regiment*
46169 *The Boy Scout*

Class 3F 0-6-0T

47267	47343	47347	47395	47528
47341	47345	47369	47400	47673

Class 8F 2-8-0

48389	48428	48500	48516
48425	48429	48501	

Class 7F 0-8-0

49428	49439

Total 129

48

Allocations: 1959

Class 3 2-6-2T

40076	40078	40093	40122
40077	40084	40107	

Class 2P 4-4-0

40674	40693

Class 2 2-6-2T

41217	41221

Class 2P 0-4-4T

41907 41908

Class 4 2-6-4T

42369	42381	42398	42399	42416

Class 6P5F 2-6-0

42772	42848	42889	42925	42936
42786	42858	42923	42930	42938
42814	42887	42924	42934	

Class 4F 0-6-0

44061	44349

Class 5 4-6-0

44686	44746	44751	45109	45426
44687	44748	44752	45111	
44741	44749	44827	45150	
44742	44750	44937	45302	

'Patriot' 4-6-0

45505 *The Royal Army Ordnance Corps*
45520 *Llandudno*
45530 *Sir Frank Ree*
45536 *Private W. Wood VC*
45540 *Sir Robert Turnbull*
45543 *Home Guard*

'Jubilee' 4-6-0

45578 *United Provinces*
45587 *Baroda*
45595 *Southern Rhodesia*
45631 *Tanganyika*
45638 *Zanzibar*
45644 *Howe*
45671 *Prince Rupert*
45680 *Camperdown*

'Royal Scot' 4-6-0

46106 *Gordon Highlander*
46108 *Seaforth Highlander*
46111 *Royal Fusilier*
46115 *Scots Guardsman*
46122 *Royal Ulster Rifleman*
46131 *The Royal Warwickshire Regiment*
46137 *The Prince of Wales's Volunteers (South Lancashire)*
46140 *The King's Royal Rifle Corps*
46143 *The South Staffordshire Regiment*
46153 *The Royal Dragoon*
46158 *The Loyal Regiment*
46160 *Queen Victoria's Rifleman*
46166 *London Rifle Brigade*
46169 *The Boy Scout*

Class 3F 0-6-0T

47267	47343	47356	47400
47291	47345	47369	47528
47341	47347	47395	47673

Class 8F 2-8-0

48165	48389	48465	48680
48275	48428	48500	48744

Class 7F 0-8-0

49428	49439

'Britannia' 4-6-2

70031 *Byron*
70032 *Tennyson*
70033 *Charles Dickens*
70043 *Lord Kitchener*

Total 105

9B STOCKPORT (EDGELEY)

Pre-Grouping Origin: LNWR
Gazetteer Ref: 45 A4
Closed: 1968
Shed-Codes: 9B (1948-1968)
Allocations: 1950

Class 3MT 2-6-2T

40071	40106	40138

Stockport yard in 1966 looking south. On display are a number of 'Black Five' and Class 8F locos which were common to the north-west towards the end of steam. W. Potter

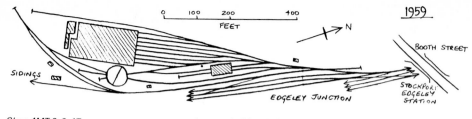

1959

BOOTH STREET

SIDINGS

EDGELEY JUNCTION

STOCKPORT
EDGELEY
STATION

FEET

Class 4MT 2-6-4T
42332 42353 42379
42352 42354 42463
Class 5MT 2-6-0
42859 42934
Class 3F 0-6-0
43281
Class 4F 0-6-0
44074 44340 44444
Class 3F 0-6-0T
47289 47346 47601
Class 7F 0-8-0T
49002 49098 49156 49281
49010 49108 49187
Class 2F 0-6-0
58377 58426

Total 27

Allocations: 1959

Class 4 2-6-4T
42316 42343 42357 42391
42322 42354 42379
Class 6P5F 2-6-0
42773 42854 42932
Class 3F 0-6-0
43192 43305 43410
Class 4F 0-6-0
44059 44075 44340 44382
Class 3F 0-6-0T
47289 47336 47346 47392 47601
Class 7F 0-8-0
49010 49191 49418 49453

Total 26

Allocations: 1965

Class 4MT 2-6-4T
42343 42374

Class 5MT 2-6-0
42710 42734 42849 42932 42942
42730 42772 42900 42941
Class 4F 0-6-0
44394
Class 5MT 4-6-0
44696 44867 44916 45291
44855 44868 45225 45382
'Jubilee' 4-6-0
45596 Bahamas
45632 Tonga
45654 Hood
Class 8F 2-8-0
48182 48310 48392 48744
48302 48338 48437
Class 2MT 2-6-2T
84013 84014 84026

Total 33

9C MACCLESFIELD

Pre-Grouping Origin: LNWR
Gazetteer Ref: 45 A5
Closed: 1961
Shed-Code: 9C (1948-1961)
Allocations: 1950

Macclesfield's own No 42318 on shed in 1957 (looking south). This shed with its small and sole allocation of 2-6-4T locos was hardly worthy of the rank of 9C when one considers the size of depots like 8C (Speke) and 10C (Patricroft). B. Hilton

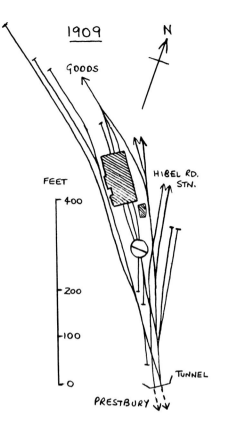

$\underline{1909}$

N

GOODS

FEET

HIBEL RD. STN.

- 400

- 200

- 100

- 0

TUNNEL

PRESTBURY

9D   BUXTON

Pre-Grouping Origin: LNWR
Gazetteer Ref: 15 A4
Closed: 1968
Shed-Codes: 9D (1948-1963)
9L (1963-1968)
Allocations: 1950(9D)

Class 2P 4-4-0

40531	40655	40692

Class 4MT 2-6-4T

42306	42318	42366	42368	42371
42315	42365	42367	42370

Class 5MT 2-6-0

42942	42943

Class 3F 0-6-0

43268	43274	43296	43562
43271	43278	43387

Class 4F 0-6-0

43842	44339	44382

Class 1P 2-4-2T

46616

Class 8F 2-8-0

48054	48326	48519	48737	48745
48090	48421	48712	48740	48746
48166	48451	48731	48741	48749
48322	48465	48734	48742

Class 7F 0-8-0

49057	49214	49348	49450
49132	49347	49387	49454

Class 4MT 2-6-4T

42319	42357	42363	42382
42355	42360	42369	42386
42356	42362	42381

Total 11

Allocations: 1959

Class 4 2-6-4T

42318	42355	42382
42348	42363	42397

Total 6

The layout of the depot was enlarged in 1935 when seven additional roads and a new turntable were provided. The extra tracks did not receive the shelter of a building and remained in the open until the closure of the depot. The other shed at Buxton was an ex-Midland Railway two road building. Its closure in 1935 was no doubt the cause of the ex-LNWR shed being enlarged to take the displaced stock. This view of 1936 shows the extra sidings and turntable.
W. Potter

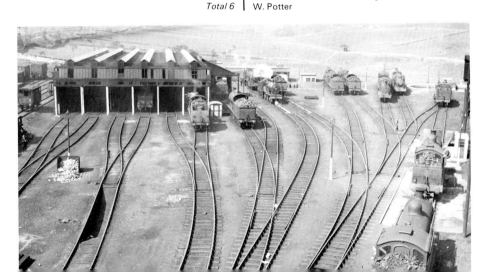

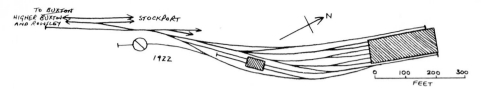

To BUXTON
HIGHER BUXTON
AND ROWSLEY
STOCKPORT

N

1922

0   100   200   300
FEET

Class 1P 0-4-4T
  58042   58084
Class 1P 2-4-0T
  58092

                    Total 55

Allocations: 1959(9D)

Class 2P 0-4-4T
  41905   41906
Class 4 2-6-4T
  42306   42370   42371
Class 6P5F 2-6-0
  42886   42942   42943
Class 3F 0-6-0
  43268   43278   43329   43538   43562
Class 4F 0-6-0
  43836   43842   44339
Class 8F 2-8-0
  48268   48322   48451   48519   48712
  48278   48421   48505   48679   48740
Class 7F 0-8-0
  48932   49281   49348   49395   49423
  49210   49315   49391   49400

                    Total 35

Allocations: 1965(9L)

Class 4F 0-6-0
  43967   44169   44310   44389   44599
  44076   44271   44339   44587
Class 2MT 2-6-0
  46401   46465   46480
Class 8F 2-8-0
  48389   48428   48464   48472
Class J94 0-6-0ST
  68006   68012   68068   68079

                    Total 20

9E   TRAFFORD PARK

Pre-Grouping Origin: Cheshire Lines Railway
Gazetteer Ref: 45 B3
Closed: 1968
Shed-Codes: 19F (1948-1949)
13A (1949)
9E (1949-1956)
17F (1957-1958)
9E (1958-1968)
Allocations: 1950(9E)

Class 3MT 2-6-2T
  40093   40094   40118
Class 4P 4-4-0
  40900   40936   41055   41076   41181
  40910   41052   41066   41154

Trafford Park shed 1952 (looking east), with a great deal of the roads exposed to the elements through a dilapidated roof. The view shows part of its unusual mixture of motive power including (left to right) a J10 0-6-0, a Compound 4-4-0, a 'Crab' 2-6-0, two 4F 0-6-0s and another compound, all in steam. Although this was the principal Cheshire Lines depot, by BR days the shed had acquired a bad reputation for filthy locos and poor maintenance. Nevertheless, closing in 1968, the depot became one of the last few in the country to play host to steam.
LGRP courtesy David & Charles

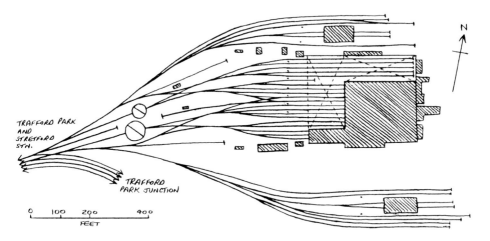

TRAFFORD PARK
AND
STRETFORD
STN.

TRAFFORD
PARK JUNCTION

N

0   100   200   400
FEET

Class 4F 0-6-0
  43896   43908   44236
Class 5MT 4-6-0
  44938
'Jubilee' 4-6-0
  45553 Canada
  45618 New Hebrides
  45622 Nyasaland
  45628 Somaliland
  45629 Straits Settlements
  45652 Hawke
Class 8F 2-8-0
  48411   48440   48680   48698
Class D16 4-4-0
  62532   62536   62587   62599
  62535   62568   62588   62609
'Director' 4-4-0
  62651 Purdon Viccars
  62653 Sir Edward Fraser
  62654 Walter Burgh Gair
  62656 Sir Clement Royds
  62657 Sir Berkeley Sheffield
  62658 Prince George
  62659 Worsley-Taylor
Class D11 4-4-0
  62670 Marne
Class J39 0-6-0
  64723   64823   64901   64954
Class J10 0-6-0
  65137   65161   65183   65201
  65141   65168   65184   65204
  65154   65179   65186
Class C12 4-4-2T
  67366   67369
Class J94 0-6-0ST
  68064
Class J67 0-6-0T
  68540   68583   68595
Class J69 0-6-0T
  68598
Class N5 0-6-2T
  69252   69326   69361
  69255   69336   69364
  69304   69343   69370

Total 73

Allocations: 1959(9E)

Class 3 2-6-2T
  40009   40018   40055   40097   40141
  40017   40052   40088   40105   40208
Class 4 2-6-4T
  42050   42336   42466   42628   42683
  42064   42419   42469   42675
  42065   42452   42479   42676
Class 3F 0-6-0
  43211   43400   43580   43587
Class 4F 0-6-0
  43846   44080   44392
  43988   44275   44402
Class 5 4-6-0
  44665   44717   44809   45239
'Jubilee' 4-6-0
  45712 Victory
Class 8F 2-8-0
  48273   48288   48741
Class 2F 0-6-0
  58213
Class J10 0-6-0
  65157   65166
'Britannia' 4-6-2
  70004 William Shakespeare
  70014 Iron Duke
  70015 Apollo
  70017 Arrow
  70021 Morning Star
  70042 Lord Roberts
Class 4 2-6-0
  76086   76088   76089

Total 53

Allocations: 1965(9E)

Class 4MT 2-6-4T
  42051   42064   42076   42113   42455
  42053   42065   42112   42230   42644
Class 5MT 4-6-0
  44673   45017   45233
  44708   45073   45269
  44735   45139   45316
  44871   45150   45352
  44895   45220   45404

Class 8F 2-8-0
48273   48288   48344   48741

Total 29

1958

9F   HEATON MERSEY

Pre-Grouping Origin: Cheshire Lines Railway
Gazetteer Ref: 45 A4
Closed: 1968
Shed-Codes: 19D (1948-1949)
13C (1949)
9F (1949-1956)
17E (1957-1958)
9F (1958-1968)
Allocations: 1950 (9F)

Class 3MT 2-6-2T
40089   40095   40113
Class 3F 0-6-0
43811
Class 4F 0-6-0
43836   44080   44144   44286   44421
43945   44090   44178   44407
Class 2MT 2-6-0
46428   46434
Class 8F 2-8-0
48089   48154   48220   48329   48676
48099   48155   48275   48406   48682
48127   48190   48315   48503   48683
48134   48208   48316   48527
Class 2F 0-6-0
58128   58282
Class D11 4-4-0
62663 *Prince Albert*
62665 *Mons*
Class J39 0-6-0
64727   64733
Class J10 0-6-0
65132   65146   65178   65193   65200*
65135   65148   56181   65194   65209
65144   56157   65185   65197
65145   65160   65188   65198
Class N5 0-6-2T
69276   69328   69332
69317   69331   69359

Total 64

Allocations: 1959 (9F)

Class 3 2-6-2T
40001   40057   40061   40089   40113
40056   40059   40067   40094   40124
Class 3F 0-6-0
43212   43245   43558   43572
Class 4F 0-6-0
43945   44261   44421
43961   44286   44501
44015   44361   44554
44090   44378
44144   44379
44236   44387
44250   44407

400

DISUSED
TURNTABLE

200

100

0
FEET

HEATON
MERSEY
SIDINGS

N

TIVIOT
DALE
STN.

CHEADLE

54

Class 8F 2-8-0

48161	48316	48429	48613	48731
48190	48317	48501	48634	
48191	48327	48503	48676	
48198	48329	48543	48677	
48208	48406	48557	48682	

Class J10 0-6-0
65194

Class 4 2-6-0

76085	76087

Total 55

Allocations: 1965 (9F)

Class 4MT 2-6-4T

42133	42134	42159

Class 4MT 2-6-0

43010	43031	43046	43063	43121
43012	43033	43047	43106	
43013	43042	43048	43120	

Class 8F 2-8-0

48089	48191	48329	48429	48613
48115	48208	48390	48501	48677
48161	48316	48403	48503	48695
48190	48327	48406	48546	48731

Total 36

9G   NORTHWICH

Pre-Grouping Origin: Cheshire Lines Railway
Gazetteer Ref: 45 C5
Closed: 1968
Shed-Codes: 13D (1949)
9G (1949-1958)
8E (1958-1968)

The shed in 1950 from the western viewpoint with Class 3F 0-6-0, Class 8F 2-8-0 and WD Class 2-8-0 locomotives on show. Heaton's own No 48134 is on the right whilst two of the J10 stud can be seen on the extreme left. LGRP courtesy David & Charles

Allocations: 1950 (9G)

Class 4F 0-6-0
44494

Class 8F 2-8-0

48045	48258	48667	48717
48046	48555	48697	48718
48135	48613	48706	48756

'Director' 4-4-0
62650 *Prince Henry*
62652 *Edwin A. Beazley*
62655 *The Earl of Kerry*

Class J11 0-6-0

64367	64453

Class J10 0-6-0

65131	65140	65158	65171	65202
65134	65147	65165	65187	65205
65138	65151	65166	65190	65208
65139	56156	65169	65191	

Class L3 2-6-4T

69052	69062

Class N5 0-6-2T

69262	69293	69335

Total 42

Northwich in 1952 with Class J10 No 65131 on the left. Facing are 'Director' class No 62651 Purdon Viccars *(then of Northwich shed) and J39 No 64901. The rear view of a Class N5 0-6-2T can also be seen as well as two other J10s. No 64901 was the only J39 to be allocated to Northwich at this time.*
LGRP courtesy David & Charles

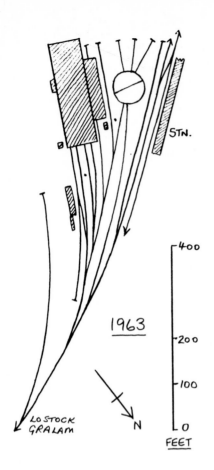

STN.

400

1963

200

100

LOSTOCK
GRALAM   N   0

FEET

10A   SPRINGS BRANCH

Pre-Grouping Origin: LNWR
Gazetteer Ref: 45 D2
Closed: 1967
Shed–Codes: 10A (1948-1958)
8F (1958-1967)
Allocations: 1950 (10A)

Class 4MT 2-6-4T
42266	42453	42456	42539	42572
42442	42454	42465	42563	42610

Class 5MT 4-6-0
45019	45235	45413	45449
45141	45313	45425	

Class 6F 0-8-2T
47877	47881	47884	47896

Class 7F 0-8-0
48895	49034	49160	49311	49394
48930	49050	49228	49331	49402
49018	49082	49264	49341	
49023	49090	49268	49352	
49024	49092	49306	49378	
49030	49129	49310	49381	

Class 2F 0-6-0
52021	52045	52051	52053

Class 3F 0-6-0
52098	52107	52126	52250	52341

Class 2F 0-6-0
58398

Total 57

Allocations: 1959 (8F)

Class 4 2-6-4T
42119	42456	42471	42666
42120	42462	42571	
42235	42465	42572	

Class 4F 0-6-0
44069	44280	44303	44438

Class 5 4-6-0
45026	45092	45313	45347	45425
45057	45135	45314	45408	45449

Class 2 2-6-0
46422	46428	46434	46448

Class 7F 0-8-0
48895	49023	49154	49311	49408
48905	49025	49155	49321	49422
48915	49049	49160	49352	49436
49007	49079	49203	49378	49438
49009	49129	49228	49381	
49018	49139	49267	49401	
49020	49150	49268	49402	

Class J10 0-6-0
65131	65138	65140	65177	65192

Class WD 2-8-0
90509	90667

Total 67

Allocations: 1965 (8F)

Class 4MT 2-6-4T
42174	42295	42587
42235	42462	42647

Allocations: 1959 (8E)

Class 4 2-6-4T
42319	42356	42386	42423

Class 4F 0-6-0
44155	44341	44375	44456

Class 8F 2-8-0
48017	48139	48297	48462	48711
48045	48155	48340	48521	48717
48046	48254	48368	48555	48742
48135	48295	48426	48605	

Class J10 0-6-0
65134	65169

Total 29

Allocations: 1965 (8E)

Class 8F 2-8-0
48118	48221	48631	48683	48735
48135	48462	48639	48693	48764
48155	48615	48640	48717	

Class 3MT 2-6-0
77011	77014

Total 16

By 1950, the shed was in a dilapidated condition and was thus entirely rebuilt. This 1953 view of Springs Branch shows two ex-LYR veterans on display, Classes 3F No 52098 and 2F No 52021. In 1952 the depot acquired Wigan Lower Ince's allocation of J10 locos with the closure of that depot.   A. G. Ellis

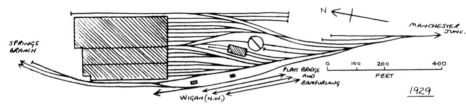

Class 5MT 2-6-0				
42948	42954	42960	42963	42977
42953	42959	42961	42968	

Class 4F 0-6-0

44490	44500

Class 5MT 4-6-0

44779	45024	45221	45314	45408
44823	45070	45278	45372	45425
44918	45108	45281	45375	45431
45019	45140	45296	45385	45449

Class 2MT 2-6-0

46402	46447	46486	46517
46419	46484	46487	

Class 3F 0-6-0T

47314	47444	47493	47603	47671

Class 8F 2-8-0

48125	48261	48278	48494
48187	48275	48379	48675

Class WD 2-8-0

90183

Total 58

10B   PRESTON

Pre-Grouping Origin: LNWR
Gazetteer Ref: 24 E3
Closed: 1961
Shed-Codes: 10B (1948-1958)
24K (1958-1961)
Allocations: 1950 (10B)

Class 2P 4-4-0
40565   40631
Class 5MT 4-6-0
44708   44874   44892   45332   45337
'Patriot' 4-6-0
45508
45516 The Bedfordshire and Hertfordshire
      Regiment
45519 Lady Godiva
45537 Private E. Sykes VC

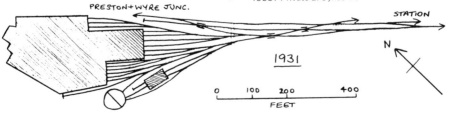

'Patriot' 4-6-0 continued
45544   45547
'Jubilee' 4-6-0
45599 Bechuanaland
Class 2MT 2-6-0
46429   46430
Class 2P 2-4-2T
46762
Class 3F 0-6-0T
47291   47293   47296   47319
Class 7F 0-8-0
49104   49141   49191   49267   49390
49134   49150   49200   49382
Class 2P 2-4-2T
50639   50676   50695
Class 0F 0-4-0ST
51218
Class 3F 0-6-0
52105   52619

Total 36

Allocations: 1959 (24K)

Class 2P 4-4-0
40565   40657   40677   40683   40694
Class 5 4-6-0
45096   45332   45340   45454
'Patriot' 4-6-0
45538 Giggleswick
45542
'Jubilee' 4-6-0
45582 Central Provinces
45633 Aden
Class 0F 0-4-0ST
47008
Class 3F 0-6-0T
47293   47319   47360   47413   47472
Class 7F 0-8-0
49104   49141   49196   49382   49396
Class 2 2-6-0
78036   78037

Total 26

This 1962 view of Preston shows the condition of the roof after the fire of June 1961. After its closure in the same year the depot continued to be used for storage purposes. On show are 'Patriot' No 45507 Royal Tank Corps and 0-8-0 No 49344. The fire not only claimed the shed roof, and ultimately the early demise of the depot, but also damaged a number of locos including Preston's own Nos 49104, 49382 and 78037. At the time it was reported that the heat was so intense it buckled a number of rails inside the building.   F. Dean

10C   PATRICROFT

Pre-Grouping Origin: LNWR
Gazetteer Ref: 45 B3
Closed: 1968
Shed-Codes: 10C (1948-1958)
26F (1958-1963)
9H (1963-1968)
Allocations: 1950(10C)

Class 2P 4-4-0
40434   40450   40628   40635
Class 4MT 2-6-4T
42560   42561   42574   42662
Class 5MT 4-6-0
45026   45142   45259   45329   45408
45037   45147   45290   45373   45410
45042   45182   45302   45377   45411
45055   45188   45304   45378   45420
45135   45199   45312   45401   45421
45137   45231   45327   45403   45424

In 1967 looking north-east towards the new westerly building consisting of eight lanes. This part of the depot was rebuilt in BR days, the diagram shows the reduced size of the building prior to completion of the operation.   M. R. Stubbs

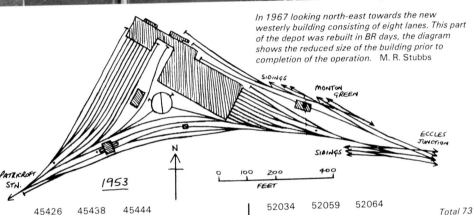

1953

| 45426 | 45438 | 45444 |
| 45428 | 45442 | 45495 |

'Jubilee' 4-6-0
45559 *British Columbia*
45563 *Australia*
45600 *Bermuda*
45668 *Madden*
45720 *Indomitable*

Class 7F 0-8-0

48920	49094	49234	49386
48926	49178	49254	49400
49027	49199	49335	49421
49087	49209	49340	49426

Class 2F 0-6-0

| 52016* | 52022 | 52024 | 52030 | 52031 |

*Ex-LYR 'Barton Wright' 0-6-0 No 52016 met with an accident in 1956 being run into by a WD 2-8-0 at this depot. In this year it was one of two survivors of the entire, once numerous, class and thus the pride of the shed. As a result of the mishap it was withdrawn from service leaving the last example of the class No 52044 allocated to Wakefield.

| 52034 | 52059 | 52064 |

Total 73

Allocations: 1959(26F)

Class 2P 4-4-0
| 40631 | 40671 |

Class 2 2-6-2T
41287

Class 4 2-6-4T

| 42442 | 42468 | 42494 | 42563 | 42662 |
| 42458 | 42478 | 42561 | 42574 | |

Class 5 4-6-0

44708	45129	45294	45378	45440
44747	45133	45304	45411	45442
44808	45182	45352	45420	
45095	45199	45377	45424	

'Jubilee' 4-6-0
45558 *Manitoba*
45559 *British Columbia*
45563 *Australia*
45600 *Bermuda*
45645 *Collingwood*
45668 *Madden*

Class 3F 0-6-0T
47284	47365	47401	47621
47309	47378	47430	47672
47364	47399	47491	

Class 7F 0-8-0
48926	49119	49209	49335	49426
49027	49147	49234	49340	
49034	49149	49249	49386	
49087	49199	49323	49421	

Class 3F 0-6-0
52201

Class 2F 0-6-0
58279

Class 5 4-6-0
73030	73126	73129	73132
73044	73127	73130	73133
73125	73128	73131	73134

Total 78

Allocations: 1965(9H)

Class 4MT 2-6-4T
42468

Class 5MT 4-6-0
44888	44926	44949	45026	45077

Class 3F 0-6-0T
47378   47647

Class 8F 2-8-0
48181	48491	48636	48714	48745
48213	48553	48663	48720	48770

Class 5MT 4-6-0
73006	73128	73134	73140	73158
73010	73129	73135	73141	73160
73011	73130	73136	73142	73163
73125	73131	73137	73143	73165
73126	73132	73138	73144	
73127	73133	73139	73157	

Class 3MT 2-6-2T
82000	82003	82009	82031	82034

Total 51

10D   PLODDER LANE

Pre-Grouping Origin: LNWR
Gazetteer Ref: 24 F1
Closed: 1954
Shed-Code: 10D (1948-1954)
Allocations: 1950

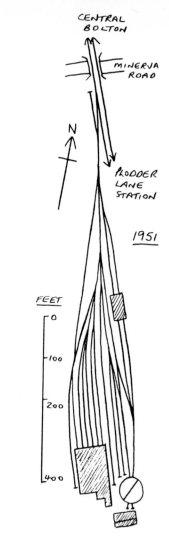

Looking south in 1947, just a few months before Nationalisation. The closure of the Bolton-Worsley line in 1954 forced the demise of this small six-road depot in the same year.   C. H. S. Owen

Class 2MT 2-6-2T
41212   41214   41216
41213   41215   41217
Class 4F 0-6-0
44237   44356   44454
44261   44384   44473
Class 3F 0-6-0T
47401
Class 7F 0-8-0
49101   49147   49315
Class 2P 2-4-2T
50644

Total 17

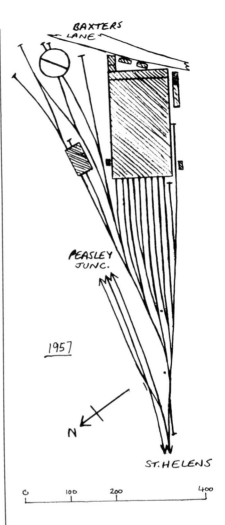

10E   SUTTON OAK

Pre-Grouping Origin: LNWR
Gazetteer Ref: 45 D3
Closed: 1967
Shed-Codes: 10E (1948-1955)
10D (1955-1958)
8G (1958-1967)
Allocations: 1950(10E)

Class 3MT 2-6-2T
40080   40084   40108
Class 4MT 2-6-0
43026   43027   43028   43029
Class 4F 0-6-0
44379
Class 1P 2-4-2T
46628   46643   46658   46727
'Sentinel' 0-4-0T
47180   47181
Class 3F 0-6-0T
47393   47444   47451   47453
Class 7F 0-8-0
49205   49262   49312   49377   49389
Class 2F 0-6-0ST
51316   51319   51397   51471   51491
Class 3F 0-6-0
52091   52280   52366   52397
52177   52349   52393   52449
Class 2F 0-6-0
58394   58410
Class 2F 0-6-2T
58900

Total 39

An overall view of the depot in 1961 looking
eastwards.   W. T. Stubbs

Allocations: 1959(8G)

Class 2 2-6-2T
41211   41286   41288   41289
Class 4 2-6-0
43022
Class 3F 0-6-0
43185   43213   43258   43294   43506
Class 4F 0-6-0
44192   44266   44300   44317   44350
Class 3F 0-6-0T
47298   47393   47452
47366   47444   47453
Class 7F 0-8-0
49262   49288   49304   49448
Class 2F 0-6-0ST
51441
Class 4 2-6-0
76075   76076   76077   76078   76079

Total 31

Allocations: 1965 (8G)

Class 2MT 2-6-2T
41286
Class 4F 0-6-0
44075   44086   44350
Class 3F 0-6-0T
47298   47377   47453
47367   47393   47668
Class 8F 2-8-0
48033   48479   48647
48326   48623   48727
Class 4MT 2-6-0
76076   76078   76080   76082   76084
76077   76079   76081   76083
Class WD 2-8-0
90178   90212   90390   90702

Total 29

10F   WIGAN LOWER INCE

Pre-Grouping Origin: GCR
Gazetteer Ref: 45 D2
Closed: 1952
Shed-Codes: 13G (1949)
10F (1949-1952)
Allocations: 1950(10F)

Class J10 0-6-0
65128   65164   65175   65196
65129   65170   65176   65199
65162   65173   65189   65203

Total 12

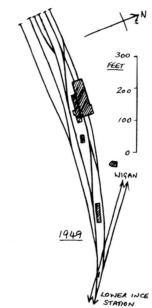

Lower Ince depot in 1939 with J10 No 5123 at the western end. W. Potter

The north end of the depot in 1967 showing (left to right) 'Black Five' No 45107, 'Britannia' No 70023, Venus (nameplates removed) and 9F No 92029. This depot has survived today in the form of 'Steamtown', the well known home of many preserved engines. Closing in August 1968 the depot was one of the last three steam venues on BR.   F. Dean

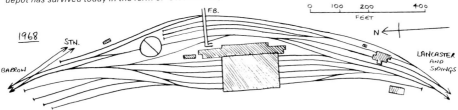

11A   CARNFORTH

Pre-Grouping Origin: LNWR
Gazetteer Ref: 24 B3
Closed: 1968
Shed-Codes: 11A (1948-1958)
24L (1958-1963)
10A (1963-1968)
Allocations: 1950(11A)

Class 3MT 2-6-2T
40041   40068   40070

Class 4MT 2-6-4T
42428   42432   42573   42615
42429   42544   42601

Class 4F 0-6-0
44060   44192   44385   44510
.44075   44374   44399

Class 5MT 4-6-0
44709   45039   45193   45333   45392
44904   45050   45306   45343   45427

Class 3F 0-6-0T
47317   47406   47410
47339   47409   47605

Class 7F 0-8-0
49109   49112   49130   49151   49241

49252   49257   49314   49438

Total 42

Allocations: 1959(24L)

Class 3 2-6-2T
40041   40081

Class 4 2-6-4T
42432   42591

Class 3F 0-6-0
43240

Class 4F 0-6-0
44306   44399   44454   44469   44510

Class 5 4-6-0
44709   45014   45054   45241   45327
44874   45017   45072   45291   45427
44892   45019   45097   45303
44904   45037   45193   45306
44905   45046   45230   45326

Class 3F 0-6-0T
47317   47342   47406   47410
47339   47373   47409

Class 7F 0-8-0
49130   49252   49449

Total 42

Allocations: 1965(10A)

Class 4MT 2-6-4T
42147   42198   42613
42154   42322

63

Class 4MT 2-6-0
| 43011 | 43036 | 43066 | 43103 |
| 43027 | 43045 | 43095 | 43105 |

Class 4F 0-6-0
| 44300 | 44386 |

Class 5MT 4-6-0
44709	44892	45054	45209	45328
44733	44904	45072	45227	45390
44778	44905	45092	45230	45399
44874	44948	45095	45326	45495

Class 3F 0-6-0T
| 47362 | 47531 | 47599 | 47662 |

Class 8F 2-8-0
| 48519 | 48712 |

Total 41

11B BARROW

Pre-Grouping Origin: Furness Railway
Gazetteer Ref: 24 B5
Closed: 1966
Shed-Codes: 11B (1948-1958)
11A (1958-1960)
12E (1960-1963)
12C (1963-1966)

Allocations: 1950 (11B)

Class 2P 4-4-0
40654

Class 2MT 2-6-2T
41221

Class 4MT 2-6-4T
42179	42372	42395	42462	42581
42321	42392	42401	42493	
42359	42393	42402	42571	

Class 4F 0-6-0
| 44059 | 44347 | 44368 | 44511 |
| 44306 | 44351 | 44487 | 44594 |

Class 5MT 4-6-0
| 44905 | 45054 | 45317 | 45386 |
| 45046 | 45291 | 45383 | |

Class 3F 0-6-0T
| 47287 | 47322 | 47323 |

Class 2P 2-4-2T
50643

Class 2F 0-6-0
58115	58199	58335	58350
58120	58291	58340	58352
58121	58299	58346	58354
58187	58309	58349	58360

Total 50

Allocations: 1959 (11A)

Class 2P 4-4-0
| 40654 | 40695 |

Looking west to the depot
in 1965, a year before steam closure.
The shed adjoined the ex-Furness Railway
works close to Barrow Docks. M. S. Houlgrave

Class 4 2-6-4T

42179	42332	42376	42401	42427
42233	42364	42392	42402	42581

Class 4F 0-6-0

43904	44347	44366	44487	44594
44086	44351	44443	44511	

Class 5 4-6-0

44837	45141	45236	45383	45386

Class 3F 0-6-0T

47287	47503	47518	47564	47676
47322	47505	47520	47605	
47323	47517	47531	47675	

Class 2F 0-6-0

58115	58120	58177	58217	58291
58116	58123	58190	58221	

Total 48

Allocations: 1965 (12C)

Class 4MT 2-6-4T

42119	42432	42610	42673	42697

Class 4F 0-6-0

44200	44443	44601

Class 5MT 4-6-0

44882	45182	45294	45383	45451
45141	45258	45340	45445	

Class 2MT 2-6-0

46400	46499

Class 3F 0-6-0T

47614	47675

Total 21

11C   OXENHOLME

Pre-Grouping Origin: LNWR
Gazetteer Ref: 24 A3
Closed: 1962
Shed-Codes: 11D (1948-1950)
11C (1950-1960)
12G (1960-1962)
Allocations: 1950 (11C)

Class 4MT 2-6-4T

42301	42314	42457	42613
42313	42317	42464	

Class 3F 0-6-0T

47503

Total 8

Class 3F 0-6-0T No 47503 simmers at the shed in 1951 still wearing the LMS lettering on its tanks. This loco was the sole 'Jinty' of the 1950 allocation. Oxenholme provided bankers for the northbound traffic up Grayrigg Bank. Its other duties included the Kendal goods shunt and the Windermere branch passenger and freight. Upon closure all the locos and men were transferred to Carnforth depot.
H. C. Casserley

Allocations: 1959 (11C)

Class 4 2-6-4T

42301	42314	42345	42464
42313	42317	42457	42613

Total 8

11D   TEBAY

Pre-Grouping Origin: LNWR
Gazetteer Ref: 27 F1
Closed: 1968
Shed-Codes: 11E (1948-1950)
11D (1950-1960)
12H (1960-1963)
12E (1963-1968)
Allocations: 1950 (11D)

Class 3MT 2-6-2T

40016	40067

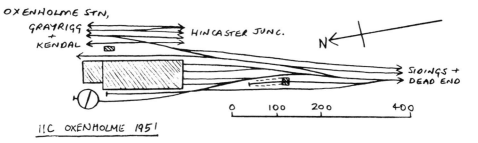

OXENHOLME STN,
GRAYRIGG
+
KENDAL

HINCASTER JUNC.

N

SIDINGS +
DEAD END

0   100   200   400

11C OXENHOLME 1951

Class 4 2-6-4T No 42110 at the shed in 1963 awaiting its next duty. The rebuilt four-lane structure should be compared to the original LNWR layout in the diagram. W. Potter

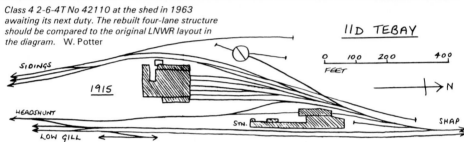

11D TEBAY

SIDINGS

1915

0   100   200   400
FEET

→N

HEADSHUNT

STN.

SHAP

LOW GILL

Class 4MT 2-6-4T
42396   42403   42404   42424
Class 4F 0-6-0
44083   44292   44459   44469

Total 10

Allocations: 1959 (11D)

Class 4 2-6-4T
42393   42396   42403   42404   42424
Class 4 2-6-0
43011   43028   43029   43035
Class 4F 0-6-0
44083   44345

Total 11

Allocations: 1965 (12E)

Class 4MT 2-6-4T
42095   42210   42232
42110   42225   42439
Class 4MT 2-6-0
43009   43029   43035

Total 9

Tebay shed is well remembered for its role in assisting struggling expresses up the famous Shap Fell by the supply of banking engines to the rear of the trains. Class 4 2-6-4Ts were most often employed and two in tandem would frequently assist the more heavier workings.

12A   CARLISLE UPPERBY

Pre-Grouping Origin: LNWR
Gazetteer Ref: 26 C1
Closed: 1966
Shed-Codes: 12B (1948-1950)
12A (1950-1958)
12B (1958-1966)
Allocations: 1950 (12A)

Class 2P 4-4-0
40356   40448   40652   40699
Class 4F 0-6-0
44081   44121   44346   44390
Class 5MT 4-6-0
44869   45129   45258   45345   45412
44871   45133   45293   45348   45414
44876   45139   45295   45351   45416
44936   45197   45296   45368   45439
44939   45230   45299   45371   45445
45065   45244   45311   45388   45451
45106   45246   45323   45409   45494
'Patriot' 4-6-0
45505 Royal Army Ordnance Corps
45512 Bunsen
45517
45518 Bradshaw
45525 Colwyn Bay
45526 Morecambe & Heysham
45542
45549

Class 8F No 48473 on the turntable of the 32-road roundhouse at Upperby in 1951. A Warrington (8B) loco, it most probably worked in with a long-haul freight to Upperby yard from the north-west. In 1963 the shed began to decline in importance after most of its freight duties transferred to Kingmoor (68A) depot. Towards the end of steam most of the 'Britannia' Pacifics spent their last years at these two depots   H. C. Casserley

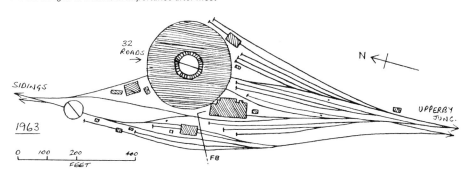

32 ROADS

SIDINGS

N

UPPERBY JUNC.

1963

F8

| 0 | 100 | 200 | 400 |
FEET

45550	45551

'Jubilee' 4-6-0
45552 *Silver Jubilee*
45555 *Quebec*
45578 *United Provinces*
45595 *Southern Rhodesia*
45624 *St Helena*
45630 *Swaziland*
45677 *Beatty*
45687 *Neptune*
'Royal Scot' 4-6-0
46110 *Grenadier Guardsman*
46136 *The Border Regiment*
46147 *The Northants Regiment*
46163 *Civil Service Rifleman*
'Coronation' 4-6-2
46225 *Duchess of Gloucester*
46226 *Duchess of Norfolk*
46228 *Duchess of Rutland*
46229 *Duchess of Hamilton*
46254 *City of Stoke-on-Trent*
46255 *City of Hereford*
Class 3F 0-6-0T

| 47295 | 47327 | 47377 | 47403 | 47415 |
| 47326 | 47340 | 47391 | 47408 | 47556 |

47614	47618	47664	47666

Class 2F 0-6-0

| 58376 | 58419 | | |

Total 87

Allocations: 1959 (12B)

Class 2P 4-4-0

| 40628 | 40629 | 40656 | | |

Class 4 2-6-4T

| 42426 | 42449 | 42539 | 42594 | 42664 |

Class 4F 0-6-0

| 43896 | 44060 | 44121 | 44326 | 44596 |
| 44016 | 44081 | 44126 | 44346 | |

Class 5 4-6-0

44770	45185	45293	45329	45412
44936	45197	45295	45344	45414
44939	45244	45296	45351	45431
45025	45246	45297	45368	45437
45070	45248	45315	45371	45438
45106	45258	45316	45394	45445
45112	45259	45317	45397	45451
45140	45286	45323	45402	45494

'Patriot' 4-6-0
45502 *Royal Naval Division*
45507 *Royal Tank Corps*

'Patriot' 4-6-0 continued
45508
45512 Bunsen
45513
45524 Blackpool
45526 Morecambe & Heysham
45533 Lord Rathmore
45537 Private E. Sykes VC
45541 Duke of Sutherland
45551
'Jubilee' 4-6-0
45588 Kashmir
45593 Kolhapur
45599 Bechuanaland
45617 Mauritius
45672 Anson
45723 Fearless
'Royal Scot' 4-6-0
46126 Royal Army Service Corps
46136 The Border Regiment
46141 The North Staffordshire Regiment
46165 The Ranger (12th London Regiment)
46167 The Hertfordshire Regiment
'Coronation' 4-6-2
46226 Duchess of Norfolk
46236 City of Bradford
46237 City of Bristol
46238 City of Carlisle
46244 King George VI
46250 City of Lichfield
46255 City of Hereford
46255 City of Salford
Class 2 2-6-0
46449   46457
Class 3F 0-6-0T
47288   47326   47377   47492   47666
47292   47337   47408   47602
47295   47340   47415   47614
Class 2F 0-6-0
58215

Total 103

Allocations: 1965 (12B)

Class 2MT 2-6-2T
41217   41222   41264   41285
Class 4F 0-6-0
44081   44390
Class 5MT 4-6-0
44937   44939   45081   45371
Class 2MT 2-6-0
46426   46434   46455   46458
'Britannia' 4-6-2
70011 Hotspur
70013 Oliver Cromwell
70022 Tornado
70029 Shooting Star
70032 Tennyson
70048 The TA 1908-58
70049 Solway Firth

Total 21

12B   CARLISLE CANAL

Pre-Grouping Origin: North British Railway
Gazetteer Ref: 26 C1
Closed: 1963
Shed-Codes: 12B (1950-1951)
68E (1951-1958)
12D (1958)
12C (1958-1963)

Looking towards the shed in 1963 past the coaling
tower which was added in LMS days. The shed was
sandwiched between the River Eden to the north and
the ex-NBR Carlisle-Silloth branch to the south. An
unusual feature of this roundhouse depot in 1925
was the additional, exterior, turntable.   W. Potter

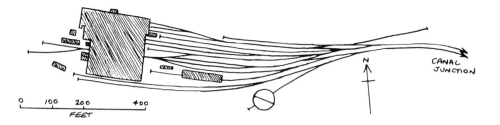

```
0    100   200      400
|___|___|___|_____|
        FEET
```

CANAL JUNCTION

N

Allocations: 1950 (12B)

Class 2P 4-4-0
  40673
Class 5MT 4-6-0
  45014   45096   45454
Class 8F 2-8-0
  48074   48323   48544
Class A3 4-6-2
  60068 *Sir Visto*
  60079 *Bayardo*
  60093 *Coronach*
  60095 *Flamingo*
Class B1 4-6-0
  61217   61219   61222
Class K3 2-6-0
  61851   61858   61898   61937
  61854   61882   61936
Class D31 4-4-0
  62281
Class D49 4-4-0
  62730 *Berkshire*
  62731 *Selkirkshire*
  62732 *Dumfries-shire*
  62734 *Cumberland*
  62735 *Westmorland*
Class J35 0-6-0
  64478   64499   64511   64526
Class J39 0-6-0
  64875   64884   64899   64932
  64877   64888   64912   64948
  64880   64895   64930   64964
Class J36 0-6-0
  65216 *Byng*
  65293
  65304
  65312
  65321
Class C15 4-4-2T
  67458   67474   67481
Class J69 0-6-0T
  68499
Class N15 0-6-2T
  69139   69174   69197   69218
  69155   69185   69215

Total 59

Allocations: 1959 (12C)

Class 4 2-6-0
  43139
Class 4F 0-6-0
  44157
Class A3 4-6-2
  60068 *Sir Visto*
  60079 *Bayardo*

  60093 *Coronach*
  60095 *Flamingo*
Class B1 4-6-0
  61064   61222   61290
  61217   61239   61395
Class K3 2-6-0
  61851   61882   61936
  61858   61916   61937
Class D49 4-4-0
  62734 *Cumberland*
  62747 *The Percy*
Class J35 0-6-0
  64478   64499
Class J39 0-6-0
  64733   64884   64895   64932
  64877   64888   64899   64948
  64880   64892   64912   64964
Class J36 0-6-0
  65237   65293   65312   65321
Class N15 0-6-2T
  69155   69215
Class N2 0-6-2T
  69564

Total 41

It should be pointed out that the A3 allocation at Canal remained unchanged until the eventual withdrawal of the above locos in the early 1960s. Also interesting to note was that J36 65321 upon its demise in 1962 had spent no less than 38 continuous years at the shed.

At closure the locos and men were transferred to Kingmoor and Upperby.

12C PENRITH

Pre-Grouping Origin: LNWR
Gazetteer Ref: 27 E1
Closed: 1962
Shed-Codes: 12C (1948-1955)
12B (1955-1958)
Allocations: 1950 (12C)

Class 4F 0-6-0
  44086
Class 2MT 2-6-0
  46449   46455
Class 2F 0-6-0
  58389   58409   58412

Total 6

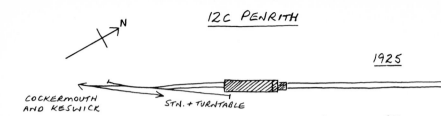

12C PENRITH

1925

COCKERMOUTH
AND KESWICK

STN. + TURNTABLE

STN.

```
0      100    200         400
|_____|_____|_____|
          FEET.
```

12D   WORKINGTON

An Ivatt Mogul from the depot No 46449, is seen on
the pits in 1951. Penrith lost its allocation by 1955,
its code in 1958 and closed completely in 1962.
H. C. Casserley

Pre-Grouping Origin: LNWR
Gazetteer Ref: 26 E3
Closed: 1968
Shed-Codes: 12D (1948-1955)
12C (1955-1958)
11B (1958-1960)
12F (1960-1963)
12D (1963-1968)
Allocations: 1950 (12D)

Class 2P 4-4-0			
40656	40694	40695	
Class 4MT 2-6-0			
43006	43007	43008	43009
Class 4F 0-6-0			
44064	44365	44495	44593
44364	44449	44505	
Class 2MT 2-6-0			
46447	46448	46456	
Class 3F 0-6-0T			
47290	47292	47593	
Class 3F 0-6-0			
52501	52508	52509	
Class 2F 0-6-0			
58362	58396	58418	58421

Total 27

12D WORKINGTON, 1959.

```
0    100   200   300
|_____|_____|_____|
       FEET
```

WORKINGTON
MAIN STATION

N

WHITEHAVEN

WAGON
WORKS

The shed in 1963 looking north. The shed was
rebuilt in 1954.   M. S. Houlgrave

Allocations: 1959 (11B)

Class 4 2-6-0
43004   43006   43008   43009   43025

Class 4F 0-6-0
43868   44360   44449   44505
44292   44365   44461   44549
44343   44390   44495

Class 2 2-6-0
46432   46447   46456   46489
46433   46455   46488   46491

Class 3F 0-6-0T
47290   47390   47593   47662
47361   47525   47604

Total 31

Allocations: 1965 (12D)

Class 4MT 2-6-0
43006   43008   43025

Class 4F 0-6-0
43953   44160   44449   44505
43964   44346   44462   44536
44157   44356   44489   44597

Class 2MT 2-6-0
46432   46488   46491

Class 3F 0-6-0T
47279   47373   47612   47676

Total 22

12E   MOOR ROW

Pre-Grouping Origin: LNW/Furness Joint Railway
Gazetteer Ref: 26 F3
Closed: 1954
Shed-Code: 12E (1948-1954)
Allocation: 1950

Class 4F 0-6-0
44461   44549

Class 3F 0-6-0T
47337   47390   47525   47604

Class 3F 0-6-0
52201   52418   52499
52285   52494   52510

Total 12

The shed in 1939 with Furness and LYR 0-6-0s
sharing the roads. By BR days the accommodation
was reduced to two lanes as the left half of the shed
had been demolished. In the year of closure it was
reported that the structure was in need of a new
roof.   W. Potter

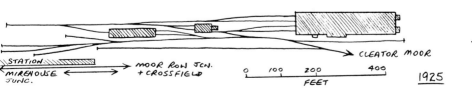

STATION
MIREHOUSE
JUNC.

MOOR ROW JCN.
+ CROSSFIELD

CLEATOR MOOR

0   100   200   400
FEET

1925

N

ROMFORD

SOUTHEND

1920

STN.

N

0   100   200   400
FEET

*This view of Upminster in the year of closure depicts
a single road structure as opposed to the original two
lane site of LTS days outlined in the diagram.
Between 1949 and closure the depot was a sub of
33A (Plaistow).* British Rail

13E   UPMINSTER

Pre-Grouping Origin: London Tilbury & Southend
Railway
Gazetteer Ref: 5 A5
Closed: 1956
Shed-Code: 13E (1948-1949)
Allocation: 1954 (33A SUB)

Class 1P 0-4-4T
  58062   58065   58091

Total 3

14A   CRICKLEWOOD

Pre-Grouping Origin: Midland Railway
Gazetteer Ref: 39 A4
Closed: 1964
Shed-Codes: 14A (1948-1963)
14B (1963-1964)
Allocations: 1950 (14A)

*A Beyer-Garratt stands near the entrance to the
southerly roundhouse in 1935. Although the depot
closed officially in 1964 it carried on servicing steam
well into 1965. The shed became known as
Cricklewood West (14B) in 1963 upon the opening
of the diesel depot which then acquired the 14A
code. The three J39s in the 1950 allocation arrived
at Cricklewood in 1949 for trials and did not depart
until early 1952!* W. Potter

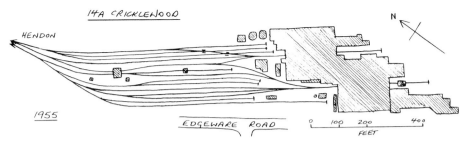

14A CRICKLEWOOD

HENDON

1955

EDGEWARE ROAD

N

0   100   200   400
FEET

Class 3MT 2-6-2T
40023   40030   40098   40172
40025   40091   40155
Class 2MT 2-6-2T
41207   41208
Class 1F 0-6-0T
41695   41712   41811
Class 5MT 2-6-0
42759   42774   42839
42771   42794   42855
Class 3F 0-6-0
43261   43313   43440   43565   43801
43307   43400   43448   43629
Class 4F 0-6-0
43901   43962   44051   44259   44581
43905   43982   44131   44297
43934   44028   44139   44304
43947   44029   44195   44529
Class 3F 0-6-0T
47203   47210   47217   47226   47433
47204   47211   47218   47227   47434
47205   47212   47219   47228   47435
47206   47213   47220   47240
47207   47214   47221   47243
47208   47215   47224   47248
47209   47216   47225   47251
Class 8F 2-8-0
48109   48163   48414   48541
48132   48410   48415
Class 2F 0-6-0
58161   58200   58235   58274
Class J39 0-6-0
64732   64918   64966

Total 89

Allocations: 1959 (14A)

Class 3 2-6-2T
40023
Class 4 2-6-0
43019   43031   43118   43120   43121

Class 4F 0-6-0
43905   43947   44228   44529
43934   44029   44259   44530
43935   44051   44297   44581
Class 5 4-6-0
44774   44816   45059   45238   45335
44777   44941   45062   45274
Class 3F 0-6-0T
47210   47214   47226   47432   47434
47211   47216   47248   47433   47435
Class 8F 2-8-0
48033   48132   48376   48495
48062   48163   48381   48638
48109   48180   48414   48750
Class 9F 2-10-0
92108   92110   92111   92112   92119

Total 54

14B   KENTISH TOWN

Pre-Grouping Origin: Midland Railway
Gazetteer Ref: 40 B5
Closed: 1963
Shed Code: 14B (1948-1963)
Allocations: 1950

Class 3MT 2-6-2T
40027   40029   40032   40034   40036
40028   40031   40033   40035   40037

A view of the large ex-Midland depot in 1958
depicting the entrance of the rebuilt No 1
roundhouse as opposed to the original 'open'
turntables of Nos 2 and 3. A Class 3 2-6-2T is seen
framed in the entrance.   Photomatic

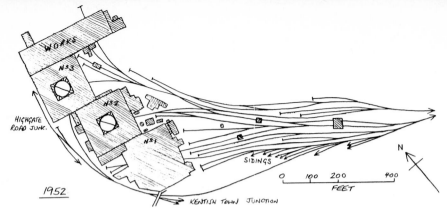

WORKS
N°3
HIGHGATE
ROAD JUNC.
N°2
N°1
SIDINGS
N

1952

0   100   200   400
FEET

KENTISH TOWN JUNCTION

Class 3MT 2-6-2T continued

40038	40099	40114	40149	40167
40079	40100	40119	40160	
40092	40111	40142	40161	
40096	40112	40148	40166	

Class 2P 4-4-0

40477	40547

Class 4P 4-4-0

40930	41020	41051	41071	41117
40932	41050	41054	41077	41199

Class 2MT 2-6-2T

41248	41249

Class 1F 0-6-0T

41661	41671	41713	41826
41664	41672	41724	

Class 4MT 2-6-4T

42133	42139	42325	42383
42138	42237	42329	

Class 4F 0-6-0

43909	44052	44298	44531
43935	44210	44397	44532
43964	44243	44440	44563

Class 5MT 4-6-0

44658	44817	44981	45253	45279
44777	44822	44984	45267	45285
44816	44846	44985	45277	

'Jubilee' 4-6-0

45557 *New Brunswick*
45598 *Basutoland*
45609 *Gilbert and Ellice Islands*
45612 *Jamaica*
45614 *Leeward Islands*
45615 *Malay States*
45616 *Malta GC*
45627 *Sierra Leone*
45641 *Sandwich*
45648 *Wemyss*
45649 *Hawkins*
45650 *Blake*
45654 *Hood*
45657 *Tyrwhitt*
45665 *Lord Rutherford of Nelson*

Class 3F 0-6-0T

47200	47245	47428
47202	47246	47429
47229	47260	47644
47241	47262	47645
47242	47282	
47244	47283	

Class 2F 0-6-0

58131	58158	58215	58229	58234

Total 117

Allocations: 1959

Class 3 2-6-2T

40021	40030	40034	40040	40119
40027	40031	40035	40092	40142
40028	40032	40036	40100	40160
40029	40033	40038	40111	40172

Class 2P 4-4-0

40548	40567	40580	40582

Class 4 2-6-4T

42156	42325	42338	42587	42682
42178	42329	42342	42610	42685
42237	42334	42540	42617	

Class 4F 0-6-0

43964	44235	44294	44531
44052	44243	44298	44532
44210	44270	44381	44563

Class 5 4-6-0

44658	44817	44846	45279
44663	44821	44855	45285
44810	44822	44985	45407
44812	44825	45277	45447

'Jubilee' 4-6-0

45557 *New Brunswick*
45561 *Saskatchewan*
45575 *Madras*
45579 *Punjab*
45585 *Hyderabad*
45598 *Basutoland*
45612 *Jamaica*
45614 *Leeward Islands*
45615 *Malay States*
45616 *Malta GC*
45618 *New Hebrides*
45622 *Nyasaland*
45628 *Somaliland*
45649 *Hawkins*
45652 *Hawke*

'Royal Scot' 4-6-0

46103 *Royal Scots Fusilier*
46130 *The West Yorkshire Regiment*
46133 *The Green Howards*
46148 *The Manchester Regiment*

Class 3F 0-6-0T

47200	47204	47209	47229	47260
47202	47205	47212	47241	47283

47437   47642   47644   47645
Class 2F 0-6-0
58131

Total 100

14C   ST ALBANS

Pre-Grouping Origin: Midland Railway
Gazetteer Ref: 11 F1
Closed: 1960
Shed Code: 14C (1948-1960)
Allocations: 1950

Class 3MT 2-6-2T
40022   40024   40026   40039
Class 1F 0-6-0T
41854
Class 4MT 2-6-4T
42132   42160   42300   42334
42134   42161   42302   42335
Class 3F 0-6-0
43245   43782
Class 3F 0-6-0T
47261
Class 2F 0-6-0
58310

Total 17

Allocations: 1959

Class 3 2-6-2T
40022   40025   40037
40024   40026   40039

Class 4 2-6-4T
42133   42159   42302   42341   42686
42134   42300   42335   42680
Class 4 2-6-0
43119
Class 4F 0-6-0
43873   43971   44043
Class 3F 0-6-0T
47261   47554

Total 21

15A   WELLINGBOROUGH

Pre-Grouping Origin: Midland Railway
Gazetteer Ref: 10 B1
Closed: 1966
Shed Codes: 15A (1948-1963)
15B (1963-1966)
Allocations: 1950(15A)

Class 2P 4-4-0
40353
Class 2MT 2-6-2T
41244
Class 2P 4-4-2T
41916
Class 3F 0-6-0
43193   43367   43797   43808
Class 4F 0-6-0
43861   43975   44037   44249   44575
43930   44033   44242   44574

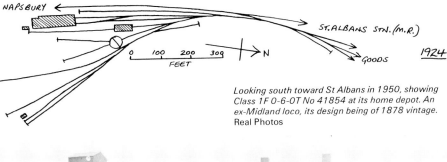

*Looking south toward St Albans in 1950, showing
Class 1F 0-6-0T No 41854 at its home depot. An
ex-Midland loco, its design being of 1878 vintage.
Real Photos*

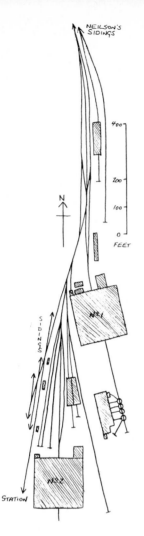

NEILSON'S SIDINGS

N

400
200
100
0
FEET

SIDINGS

No.1

SIDINGS

No.2

STATION

Class 3F 0-6-0T
47238	47273	47446	47636
47264	47279	47543	47642
47265	47333	47554	

Class 8F 2-8-0
48010	48180	48305	48378	48651
48024	48181	48334	48385	48668
48035	48183	48338	48386	48671
48050	48191	48359	48492	48678
48082	48192	48360	48533	48692
48128	48198	48363	48617	48695
48149	48222	48364	48619	48699
48150	48264	48365	48625	
48151	48269	48371	48627	
48167	48281	48374	48644	

Class 1P 0-4-4T
| 58045 | 58053 | 58085 |

Total 77

Allocations: 1959(15A)

Class 4F 0-6-0
| 43861 | 43977 | 43995 | 44182 | 44575 |
| 43929 | 43979 | 44175 | 44574 | |

Class 3F 0-6-0T
| 47265 | 47273 |

Class 8F 2-8-0
48374	48386	48625	48651	48695
48378	48492	48627	48671	48699
48385	48617	48644	48678	

Class 2 2-6-2T
| 84006 | 84007 | 84008 |

Class 9F 2-10-0
92018	92025*	92055	92084	92126
92019	92026*	92056	92085	92127
92020*	92027*	92058	92107	92132
92021*	92028*	92059	92122	92133
92022*	92029*	92080	92123	92134
92023*	92052	92082	92124	92154
92024*	92054	92083	92125	92159

Total 63

Allocations: 1965(15B)

Class 8F 2-8-0
48082	48285	48376	48530	48759
48132	48301	48381	48545	
48180	48356	48382	48609	
48183	48374	48492	48671	

Total 17

Photo shows (left to right) No 47208 (15A),
No 40461 (16A) and Nos 92022, 48678, 47265 (all
15A) inside one of the two roundhouses in 1957.
The No 1 (north) building was demolished in 1964 to
make way for a new diesel depot. C. I. K. Field

*It will be seen that the 1959 stud included the full
(92020-9) class of 'Franco Crosti' 2-10-0s.

This view of the depot was taken only months after Nationalisation in 1948 as the mixture of numberplates and the figures LMS suggest. As will be seen from the diagram the station platform gave an excellent vantage point for spotters.

H. C. Casserley

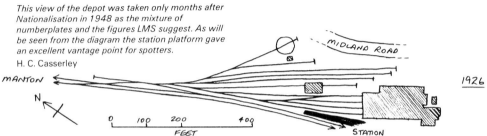

15B   KETTERING

Pre-Grouping Origin: Midland Railway
Gazetteer Ref: 10 A2
Closed: 1965
Shed Codes: 15B (1948-1963)
15C (1963-1965)
Allocations: 1950(15B)

Class 2P 4-4-0
40550
Class 4P 4-4-0
41012   41053   41063   41087
Class 4F 0-6-0
43889   43898   44043   44278   44465
Class 2MT 2-6-0
46400   46401   46402   46403   46404
Class 3F 0-6-0T
47437
Class 8F 2-8-0
48069   48143   48355   48611   48759
48124   48285   48356   48645
48141   48301   48471   48704
Class 2F 0-6-0
58162   58172   58193   58195
58164   58183   58194   58214

Total 37

Allocations: 1959(15B)

Class 6P5F 2-6-0
42764

Class 4 2-6-0
43042   43048
Class 3F 0-6-0
43249   43333   43624   43721
Class 2 2-6-0
46403   46404   46444   46495   46496
Class 8F 2-8-0
48050   48142   48313   48467   48690
48069   48143   48355   48609   48704
48124   48285   48356   48611   48759
48141   48301   48380   48645
Class 2 2-6-0
78020   78021   78028
Class 9F 2-10-0
92105   92106   92160   92163   92164

Total 39

15C   LEICESTER MIDLAND

Pre-Grouping Origin: Midland Railway
Gazetteer Ref: 16 F3
Closed: 1966
Shed Codes: 15C (1948-1963)
15A (1963-1966)
Allocations: 1950(15C)

Class 3MT 2-6-2T
40145   40146   40173   40182

The shed in 1966 about one month before steam closure. In 1952 work commenced on the rebuilding of the depot and whilst this was in progress the ex-Midland shed at Wigston (closed 1934) was used for the stabling of locos. A new coaling stage was also built as the conditions were previously primitive.   J. D. Stevenson

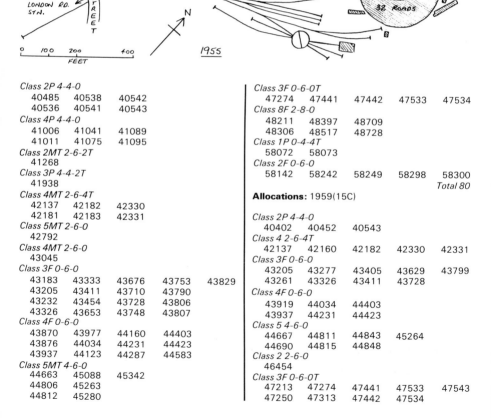

Class 2P 4-4-0
40485	40538	40542
40536	40541	40543

Class 4P 4-4-0
41006	41041	41089
41011	41075	41095

Class 2MT 2-6-2T
41268

Class 3P 4-4-2T
41938

Class 4MT 2-6-4T
42137	42182	42330
42181	42183	42331

Class 5MT 2-6-0
42792

Class 4MT 2-6-0
43045

Class 3F 0-6-0
43183	43333	43676	43753	43829
43205	43411	43710	43790	
43232	43454	43728	43806	
43326	43653	43748	43807	

Class 4F 0-6-0
43870	43977	44160	44403
43876	44034	44231	44423
43937	44123	44287	44583

Class 5MT 4-6-0
44663	45088	45342
44806	45263	
44812	45280	

Class 3F 0-6-0T
47274	47441	47442	47533	47534

Class 8F 2-8-0
48211	48397	48709
48306	48517	48728

Class 1P 0-4-4T
58072	58073

Class 2F 0-6-0
58142	58242	58249	58298	58300

Total 80

Allocations: 1959(15C)

Class 2P 4-4-0
40402	40452	40543

Class 4 2-6-4T
42137	42160	42182	42330	42331

Class 3F 0-6-0
43205	43277	43405	43629	43799
43261	43326	43411	43728	

Class 4F 0-6-0
43919	44034	44403
43937	44231	44423

Class 5 4-6-0
44667	44811	44843	45264
44690	44815	44848	

Class 2 2-6-0
46454

Class 3F 0-6-0T
47213	47274	47441	47533	47543
47250	47313	47442	47534	

78

Class 8F 2-8-0
48007	48027	48107	48149	48266
48010	48061	48133	48211	

Class 4 2-6-0
75057	75058	75059	75060	75061

Class 2 2-6-0
78029

Class 9F 2-10-0
92100	92102	92104	92121
92101	92103	92109	92128

Total 63

Allocations: 1965(15A)

Class 8F 2-8-0
48024	48165	48361	48637
48053	48185	48414	48645
48065	48212	48528	48685
48116	48279	48625	48698

Class 2MT 2-6-0
78013	78021	78027	78028	78061

Class 2MT 2-6-2T
84005	84006	84008

Total 24

15D BEDFORD

Pre-Grouping Origin: Midland Railway
Gazetteer Ref: 11 D1
Closed: 1963

Shed-Codes: 15D (1948-1958)
14E (1958-1963)
14C (1963)
Allocations: 1950 (15D)

Class 3MT 2-6-2T
40141	40165

Class 2P 4-4-0
40551

Class 3P 4-4-0
40762

Class 4P 4-4-0
41007	41038	41070	41094
41009	41044	41091	41198

Class 2MT 2-6-2T
41209	41269	41270	41271

Class 3F 0-6-0
43174	43428	43721	43777
43222	43474	43766	43785

Class 4F 0-6-0
43888	43910	43923	43967	43971

Class 3F 0-6-0T
47223	47252	47549

Class 8F 2-8-0
48177

Class 1P 0-4-4T
58040	58051	58054	58059	58091

Class 2F 0-6-0
58149	58239	58241	58305

Total 42

Allocations: 1959 (14E)

Class 3 2-6-2T
40020

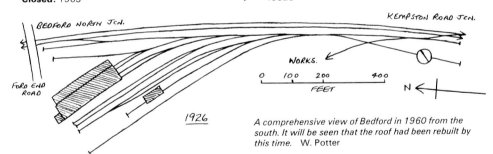

A comprehensive view of Bedford in 1960 from the south. It will be seen that the roof had been rebuilt by this time. W. Potter

Class 2 2-6-2T
41271   41280
Class 3F 0-6-0
43428   43529   43665   43808
43440   43531   43766   43829
43474   43565   43785
Class 5 4-6-0
44984   45139   45267
45137   45221   45342
Class 3F 0-6-0T
47264   47279   47549
Class 2F 0-6-0
58214
Class 4 4-6-0
75040   75042   75044
75041   75043   75055
Class 2 2-6-2T
84005

Total 31

16A NOTTINGHAM

Pre-Grouping Origin: Midland Railway
Gazetteer Ref: 41 G4
Closed: 1965
Shed-Codes: 16A (1948-1963)
16D (1963-1965)
Allocations: 1950 (16A)

Class 3MT 2-6-2T
40120   40140   40178
Class 2P 4-4-0
40415   40452   40504   40546   40560
40417   40458   40535   40552
40419   40478   40540   40553
Class 4P 4-4-0
40929   41019   41082
41015   41032   41096
Class 1F 0-6-0T
41682   41686   41846
Class 2P 4-4-2T
41917   41921   41925
41919   41922   41926

Looking west in 1937 towards the centre roundhouse with ex-LTS 4-4-2T LMS No 2101, in the foreground. This loco became BR No 41919 and was one of six of the class allocated to Nottingham in 1950. The well planned positioning of the three roundhouses enabled easy access and allowed more scope during shunting movements. H. C. Casserley

Class 4MT 2-6-4T
42140   42228   42339   42680
42184   42229   42361   42686
42185   42333   42373
Class 5MT 2-6-0
42823
Class 4MT 2-6-0
43018   43019   43033   43040
Class 3F 0-6-0
43192   43369   43401   43711
43240   43371   43538   43723
43249   43378   43558   43724
43300   43399   43637   43729
Class 4F 0-6-0
43954   44030   44095   44158   44230
43956   44039   44113   44215   44247
43958   44055   44132   44223   44264

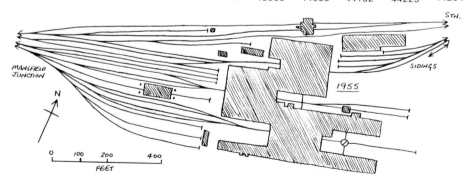

MANSFIELD JUNCTION

STN.

SIDINGS

1955

N

0   100   200   400

FEET

44313	44412	44472	44546	44585
44401	44414	44480	44577	44598
44408	44425	44533	44578	

Class 5MT 4-6-0

44773	44841	44918
44825	44861	45059

'Jubilee' 4-6-0
45554 *Ontario*
45611 *Hong Kong*
45620 *North Borneo*
45636 *Uganda*
45640 *Frobisher*

Class 3F 0-6-0T

47277	47485	47623	47632
47422	47539	47629	47637
47438	47552	47631	

Class 8F 2-8-0

48003	48206	48293	48614	48666
48064	48217	48380	48635	48675
48102	48218	48381	48639	48696
48170	48279	48402	48653	

Class 3F 0-6-0

52121	52123	52135

Class 1P 2-4-0
58020

Class 1P 0-4-4T

58050	58056

Class 2F 0-6-0

58133	58135	58201	58248	58252

Total 144

Allocations: 1959 (16A)

Class 2P 4-4-0

40411	40493	40542	40632
40421	40502	40550	
40454	40504	40557	
40487	40534	40585	

Class 4 2-6-4T

42140	42161	42185	42636

Class 4F 0-6-0

43856	43962	44132	44248	44533
43859	43972	44139	44313	44546
43888	44018	44151	44394	44555
43917	44021	44158	44401	44577
43918	44030	44195	44412	44578
43928	44033	44204	44414	44585
43954	44095	44215	44472	
43958	44131	44223	44480	

Class 5 4-6-0

44806	44861	44944	45253
44858	44918	45088	45263

'Jubilee' 4-6-0
45611 *Hong Kong*
45620 *North Borneo*
45636 *Uganda*
45641 *Sandwich*
45650 *Blake*
45667 *Jellicoe*

Class 3F 0-6-0T
47277

Class 8F 2-8-0

48000	48177	48286	48653	48763
48064	48217	48377	48666	
48108	48218	48614	48675	
48117	48261	48635	48696	
48170	48279	48639	48748	

Class 2F 0-6-0
58175

Class 4 4-6-0

75056	75062	75063	75064

Total 96

Allocations: 1965 (16D)

Class 3F 0-6-0T
47231

Total 1

16B PETERBOROUGH SPITAL BRIDGE

Pre-Grouping Origin: Midland Railway
Gazetteer Ref: 17 F2
Closed: 1960
Shed-Codes: 16B (1948-1950)
35C (1950-1958)
31F (1958-1960)

A view of the depot in 1950 looking north-west. The depot became part of the Eastern Region in 1950 when it began acquiring classes of LNER vintage. The depot was demolished in the year of closure and the site cleared. LGRP courtesy David & Charles

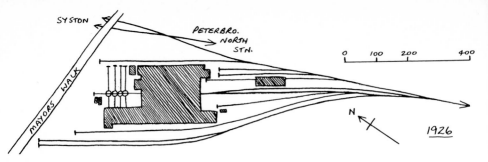

SYSTON

PETERBRO.
NORTH
STN.

MAYORS WALK

0   100   200   400

N

1926

Allocations: 1950 (35C)

Class 2P 4-4-0
40401	40482	40532	40559
40410	40497	40558	

Class 4P 4-4-0
40934	41083

Class 3F 0-6-0
43319	43651

Class 4F 0-6-0
43854	43981	44152	44273	44509
43863	44053	44155	44293	44518
43864	44097	44218	44296	44519
43957	44110	44238	44458	44521
43980	44117	44239	44476	44522

Class 3F 0-6-0T
47269	47566	47622
47270	47621	47659

Class C12 4-4-2T
67362

Total 43

Allocations: 1959 (31F)

Class 3P 4-4-2T
41949	41969	41975

Class 4 2-6-0
43127

Class 4F 0-6-0
43957	44152	44273	44518	44522
44097	44239	44476	44519	
44110	44247	44509	44521	

Class 3F 0-6-0T
47300

Class B1 4-6-0
61095	61156	61205	61348
61096	61204	61323	

Class D16 4-4-0
62597	62612	62613

Class J39 0-6-0
64789	64901

Class WD 2-8-0
90063	90447	90501	90528

Total 34

16C KIRKBY-IN-ASHFIELD

Pre-Grouping Origin: Midland Railway
Gazetteer Ref: 41 E4
Closed: 1966
Shed Codes: 16C (1948-1955)
16B (1955-1963)
16E (1963-1966)
Allocations: 1950 (16C)

Class 3F 0-6-0
43468	43494	43596	43773

The shed and yard in 1947 before the expansion with Class 8F 2-8-0s dominating the scene. The depot was enlarged in 1958 by the addition of a two road structure shown in the diagram.
LGRP courtesy David & Charles

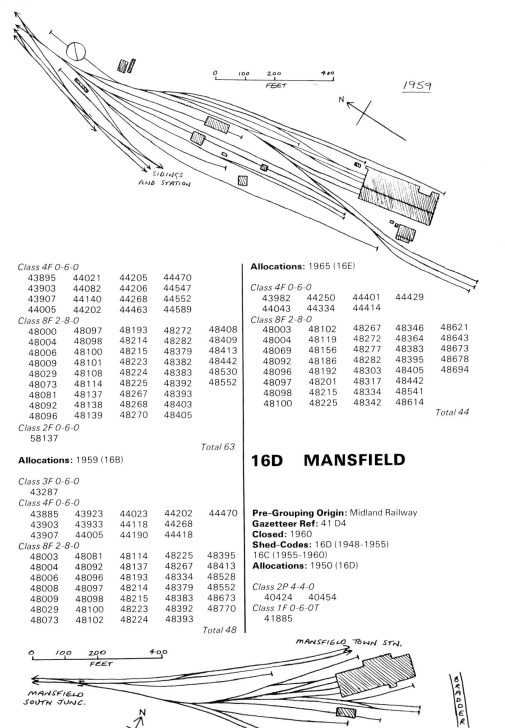

SIDINGS AND STATION

1959

Class 4F 0-6-0			
43895	44021	44205	44470
43903	44082	44206	44547
43907	44140	44268	44552
44005	44202	44463	44589

Class 8F 2-8-0				
48000	48097	48193	48272	48408
48004	48098	48214	48282	48409
48006	48100	48215	48379	48413
48009	48101	48223	48382	48442
48029	48108	48224	48383	48530
48073	48114	48225	48392	48552
48081	48137	48267	48393	
48092	48138	48268	48403	
48096	48139	48270	48405	

Class 2F 0-6-0
58137

Total 63

Allocations: 1959 (16B)

Class 3F 0-6-0
43287

Class 4F 0-6-0				
43885	43923	44023	44202	44470
43903	43933	44118	44268	
43907	44005	44190	44418	

Class 8F 2-8-0				
48003	48081	48114	48225	48395
48004	48092	48137	48267	48413
48006	48096	48193	48334	48528
48008	48097	48214	48379	48552
48009	48098	48215	48383	48673
48029	48100	48223	48392	48770
48073	48102	48224	48393	

Total 48

Allocations: 1965 (16E)

Class 4F 0-6-0			
43982	44250	44401	44429
44043	44334	44414	

Class 8F 2-8-0				
48003	48102	48267	48346	48621
48004	48119	48272	48364	48643
48069	48156	48277	48383	48673
48092	48186	48282	48395	48678
48096	48192	48303	48405	48694
48097	48201	48317	48442	
48098	48215	48334	48541	
48100	48225	48342	48614	

Total 44

16D MANSFIELD

Pre-Grouping Origin: Midland Railway
Gazetteer Ref: 41 D4
Closed: 1960
Shed-Codes: 16D (1948-1955)
16C (1955-1960)
Allocations: 1950 (16D)

Class 2P 4-4-0
40424   40454
Class 1F 0-6-0T
41885

MANSFIELD TOWN STN.

MANSFIELD SOUTH JUNC.

MANSFIELD EAST JUNC.

1958

B R A D D E R ST.

Class 3P 4-4-2T
41940	41947	41961
41943	41958	41962

Class 3F 0-6-0
43239	43522	43634
43431	43529	43727

Class 4F 0-6-0
43874	43997	44394	44416
43983	44004	44415	

Class 8F 2-8-0
48088	48156	48643
48119	48621	48701

Allocations: 1959 (16C)　　　　　　　　*Total 28*

Class 3 2-6-2T
40004	40096	40168	40184
40079	40146	40175	

Class 1F 0-6-0T
41712	41844

Class 4F 0-6-0
44252	44415	44416	44441

Class 2 2-6-0
46501

Class 8F 2-8-0
48001	48119	48277	48442	48621
48024	48156	48282	48447	48643
48088	48272	48405	48541	48701

Total 29

A 1946 view of the ex-Midland depot at Mansfield showing ex-MR Class 1P 0-4-4T LMS No 1350 and ex-LTS Class 3P 4-4-2T LMS No 2122. This latter engine became BR No 41940 and formed part of the allocation in 1950. Upon closure most of the duties and locos transferred to Kirkby in Ashfield (16C). LGRP courtesy David & Charles

17A　DERBY

Pre-Grouping Origin: Midland Railway
Gazetteer Ref: 41 G2
Closed: 1967
Shed-Codes: 17A (1948-1963)
16C (1963-1967)
Allocations: 1950 (17A)

Class 2P 4-4-0
40383	40407	40416	40426	40632
40404	40411	40418	40513	

Class 4P 4-4-0
40927	41003	41043	41059	41084
41000	41023	41057	41060	41088

Class 2MT 2-6-2T
41247

Class 0F 0-4-0T
41535

Class 1F 0-6-0T
41726	41754	41779	41833	41889
41747	41773	41795	41847	

Class 2P 0-4-4T
41903

Class 4MT 2-6-4T
42177	42340	42341

Class 5MT 2-6-0
42847	42872	42897

Class 4MT 2-6-0
43010	43031	43049

Class 3F 0-6-0
43137	43191	43226	43312	43318
43185	43200	43259	43315	43323

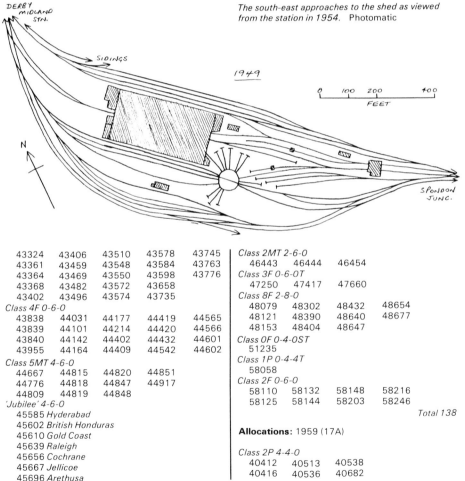

The south-east approaches to the shed as viewed from the station in 1954.   Photomatic

1949

0   100   200   400

FEET

					Class 2MT 2-6-0		
43324	43406	43510	43578	43745	46443	46444	46454
43361	43459	43548	43584	43763	*Class 3F 0-6-0T*		
43364	43469	43550	43598	43776	47250	47417	47660
43368	43482	43572	43658		*Class 8F 2-8-0*		
43402	43496	43574	43735		48079	48302	48432	48654

Class 4F 0-6-0

					48121	48390	48640	48677
43838	44031	44177	44419	44565	48153	48404	48647	
43839	44101	44214	44420	44566	*Class 0F 0-4-0ST*			
43840	44142	44402	44432	44601	51235			
43955	44164	44409	44542	44602	*Class 1P 0-4-4T*			

Class 5MT 4-6-0

58058

				Class 2F 0-6-0			
44667	44815	44820	44851	58110	58132	58148	58216
44776	44818	44847	44917	58125	58144	58203	58246
44809	44819	44848					

'Jubilee' 4-6-0

Total 138

45585 *Hyderabad*
45602 *British Honduras*
45610 *Gold Coast*
45639 *Raleigh*
45656 *Cochrane*
45667 *Jellicoe*
45696 *Arethusa*

Allocations: 1959 (17A)

Class 2P 4-4-0

40412	40513	40538
40416	40536	40682

85

Class 4P 4-4-0
40925　41062　41157

Class 1F 0-6-0T
41726　41754　41773　41847

Class 4 2-6-4T
42174　42181　42184　42326

Class 3F 0-6-0

43200	43318	43459	43584	43735
43306	43324	43510	43658	
43315	43368	43548	43727	

Class 4F 0-6-0

43840	44020	44164	44334	44428
43881	44031	44169	44369	44465
43925	44042	44176	44380	44540
43930	44048	44177	44409	44545
43955	44049	44214	44419	44601
43969	44112	44295	44420	
43991	44142	44304	44425	

Class 5 4-6-0

44688	44818	44839	44851	44856

'Jubilee' 4-6-0
45610 Ghana
45626 Seychelles
45627 Sierra Leone
45648 Wemyss
45663 Jervis

Class 2 2-6-0

46402	46443	46499	46502
46440	46497	46500	

Class OF 0-4-0ST
47000

Class 3F 0-6-0T
47563　47629　47660

Class 8F 2-8-0

48005	48121	48270	48390
48079	48153	48293	48403
48083	48168	48302	48510

Class 2F 0-6-0

58132	58144	58158	58219

Class 5 4-6-0

73135	73138	73141	73144	73159
73136	73139	73142	73157	
73137	73140	73143	73158	

Total 113

Allocations: 1965 (16C)

Class 4MT 2-6-4T
42156

Class 5MT 4-6-0

44659	44811	44861	45267
44690	44815	44920	45289
44804	44830	45190	

Class OF 0-4-0ST
47000　47006

Class 3F 0-6-0T
47534

Class 8F 2-8-0

48000	48103	48198	48359	48627
48060	48124	48270	48362	48635
48064	48149	48284	48370	48653
48073	48153	48313	48510	48666
48083	48170	48350	48604	

Class 2MT 2-6-0
78000　78020　78064

Total 42

17B　BURTON

Pre-Grouping Origin: Midland Railway
Gazetteer Ref: 15 D5
Closed: 1966
Shed-Codes: 17B (1948-1963)
16F (1963-1966)
Allocations: 1950 (17B)

Class 2P 4-4-0

40325	40395	40436	40519	40526
40364	40432	40453	40525	40633

Class 2MT 2-6-2T
41230

Class OF 0-4-0ST*
41516　41523

Class OF 0-4-0T
41536

Class 1F 0-6-0T
41748　41770　41839　41865　41878

Class 4MT 2-6-4T
42336

Class 5MT 2-6-0

42756	42763	42769	42799	42896
42761	42767	42791	42846	42922

Class 3F 0-6-0

43188	43286	43395	43623
43244	43306	43582	43652
43247	43340	43608	43709
43256	43388	43619	43815

Looking north to the shed in 1946.
LGRP courtesy David & Charles

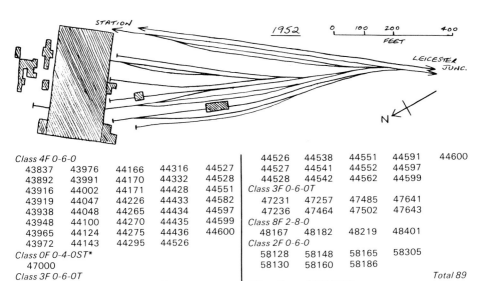

STATION 1952 0 100 200 400 FEET LEICESTER JUNC. N

Class 4F 0-6-0

43837	43976	44166	44316	44527
43892	43991	44170	44332	44528
43916	44002	44226	44428	44551
43919	44047	44265	44433	44582
43938	44048	44270	44434	44597
43948	44100	44275	44435	44599
43965	44124	44295	44436	44600
43972	44143		44526	

Class OF 0-4-0ST*
47000

Class 3F 0-6-0T

47231	47253	47464	47643
47233	47257	47641	

Classes OF 0-4-0ST*
51217 (LYR)
56020 (Cal R)

Class 1P 0-4-4T
58080   58087

Class 2F 0-6-0

58130	58186	58236	58267
58145	58207	58258	58304
58160	58221	58262	

Total 108

*In 1950, the depot possessed a great variety of shunting locomotives including five saddle tanks which alone represented four different classes from four sources, LMS, Midland, L&Y and Caledonian.

Allocations: 1959 (17B)

Class 2P 4-4-0
40396   40453   40633

Class 2 2-6-2T
41277   41328

Class OF 0-4-0T
41532   41536

Class 1F 0-6-0T
41878

Class 6P5F 2-6-0

42756	42767	42822	42826	42855
42759	42799	42824	42829	42896
42763	42818	42825	42839	42922

Class 3F 0-6-0

43188	43327	43574	43623	43709
43247	43340	43608	43652	43809
43256	43570	43621	43679	

Class 4F 0-6-0

43839	43948	43998	44168	44433
43843	43953	44047	44241	44434
43870	43976	44100	44316	44435
43880	43989	44124	44332	44436

44526	44538	44551	44591	44600
44527	44541	44552	44597	
44528	44542	44562	44599	

Class 3F 0-6-0T

47231	47257	47485	47641
47236	47464	47502	47643

Class 8F 2-8-0

48167	48182	48219	48401

Class 2F 0-6-0

58128	58148	58165	58305
58130	58160	58186	

Total 89

Allocations: 1965 (16F)

Class 5MT 4-6-0

44688	44851	44962	45224	45262
44825	44858	44989	45232	45464
44839	44941	45062	45253	

Class 3F 0-6-0T

47313	47464	47629	47643

Class 8F 2-8-0

48117	48266	48368	48672
48128	48271	48606	48690
48194	48332	48651	48700
48254	48367	48662	48728

Total 34

17C COALVILLE

Pre-Grouping Origin: Midland Railway
Gazetteer Ref: 16 E4
Closed: 1965
Shed-Codes: 17C (1948-1958)
15D (1958-1963)
15E (1963-1965)
Allocations: 1950 (17C)

Class 3F 0-6-0

43429	43682	43779	43809

Class 4F 0-6-0

43835	43894	44109	44227	44539
43865	43921	44148	44252	44554
43872	44085	44156	44260	44572
43882	44103	44180	44279	

Class 3F 0-6-0T
47449

Class 8F 2-8-0

48008	48107	48265	48475	48543

A 1950 view of the depot with a line up of Class 4F 0-6-0s. In 1963, the last three Johnson Class 2 0-6-0s Nos 58143/8/82 were shedded here to work through the restricted clearance Glenfield Tunnel. Real Photos

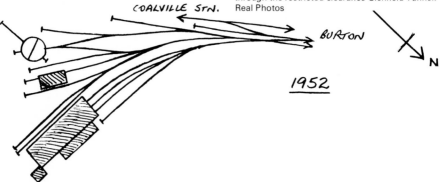

1952

Class 2F 0-6-0

58163	58174	58247	58264

Total 33

Allocations: 1959 (15D)

Class 4F 0-6-0

43854	44103	44156	44278
43876	44109	44166	44279
43975	44113	44180	44539
44085	44148	44260	44572

Class 3F 0-6-0T
47449

Class 8F 2-8-0

48053	48382	48619

Class 2F 0-6-0

58163	58209	58246	58298

Total 24

Allocations: 1965 (15E)

Class 8F 2-8-0

48063	48219	48467	48619	48699
48105	48315	48552	48644	
48107	48380	48607	48687	
48137	48388	48617	48696	

Total 17

17D ROWSLEY

Pre-Grouping Origin: Midland Railway
Gazetteer Ref: 41 C1
Closed: 1965
Shed-Codes: 17D (1948-1958)
17C (1958-1963)
16J (1963-1964)
Allocations: 1950 (17D)

Class 2P 4-4-0

40499	40520

Class 4P 4-4-0
41049

Class 1F 0-6-0T
41875

Class 5MT 2-6-0

42760	42768	42873	42874	42902

Class 3F 0-6-0

43273	43290	43342	43370

Class 4F 0-6-0

43881	43918	43925	43929	44017

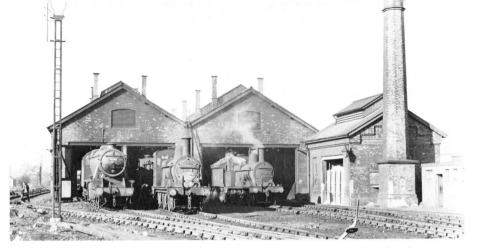

Rowsley shed lost its code in 1964 and became a sub of Derby (16C). It closed the following year and was quickly demolished. This 1949 view of the south end shows an 8F 2-8-0 and two Johnson 2F 0-6-0s

Nos (LMS) 3113 and 3043. Both these locos belonged to Rowsley and eventually received numbers prefixed with '58'. Real Photos

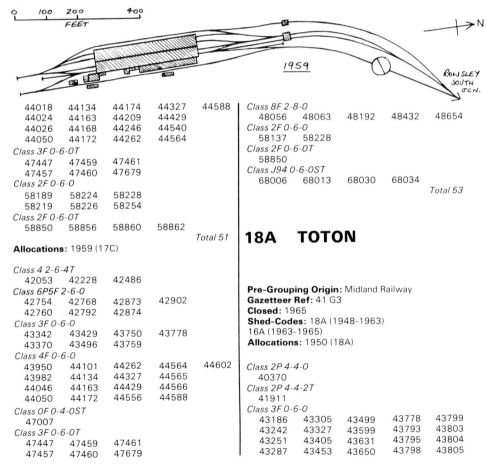

44018	44134	44174	44327	44588
44024	44163	44209	44429	
44026	44168	44246	44540	
44050	44172	44262	44564	

Class 3F 0-6-0T

| 47447 | 47459 | 47461 |
| 47457 | 47460 | 47679 |

Class 2F 0-6-0

| 58189 | 58224 | 58228 |
| 58219 | 58226 | 58254 |

Class 2F 0-6-0T

| 58850 | 58856 | 58860 | 58862 |

Total 51

Allocations: 1959 (17C)

Class 4 2-6-4T

| 42053 | 42228 | 42486 |

Class 6P5F 2-6-0

| 42754 | 42768 | 42873 | 42902 |
| 42760 | 42792 | 42874 | |

Class 3F 0-6-0

| 43342 | 43429 | 43750 | 43778 |
| 43370 | 43496 | 43759 | |

Class 4F 0-6-0

43950	44101	44262	44564	44602
43982	44134	44327	44565	
44046	44163	44429	44566	
44050	44172	44556	44588	

Class 0F 0-4-0ST

| 47007 |

Class 3F 0-6-0T

| 47447 | 47459 | 47461 |
| 47457 | 47460 | 47679 |

Class 8F 2-8-0

| 48056 | 48063 | 48192 | 48432 | 48654 |

Class 2F 0-6-0

| 58137 | 58228 |

Class 2F 0-6-0T

| 58850 |

Class J94 0-6-0ST

| 68006 | 68013 | 68030 | 68034 |

Total 53

18A TOTON

Pre-Grouping Origin: Midland Railway
Gazetteer Ref: 41 G3
Closed: 1965
Shed-Codes: 18A (1948-1963)
16A (1963-1965)
Allocations: 1950 (18A)

Class 2P 4-4-0

| 40370 |

Class 2P 4-4-2T

| 41911 |

Class 3F 0-6-0

43186	43305	43499	43778	43799
43242	43327	43599	43793	43803
43251	43405	43631	43795	43804
43287	43453	43650	43798	43805

Two Class 8F 2-8-0s at rest around one of the de-roofed roundhouses at Toton in 1948, in which year the depot underwent rebuilding. Although the depot closed in 1965, it continued in use for loco storage into 1966.   H. C. Casserley

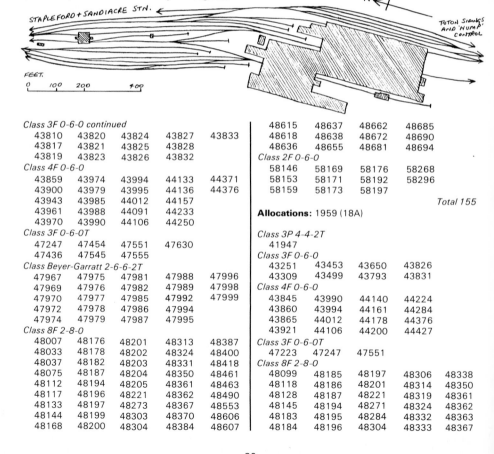

STAPLEFORD + SANDIACRE STN.

N

TOTON SIDINGS AND 'HUMP' CONTROL

FEET.
0   100   200   400

Class 3F 0-6-0 continued				
43810	43820	43824	43827	43833
43817	43821	43825	43828	
43819	43823	43826	43832	

Class 4F 0-6-0				
43859	43974	43994	44133	44371
43900	43979	43995	44136	44376
43943	43985	44012	44157	
43961	43988	44091	44233	
43970	43990	44106	44250	

Class 3F 0-6-0T			
47247	47454	47551	47630
47436	47545	47555	

Class Beyer-Garratt 2-6-6-2T				
47967	47975	47981	47988	47996
47969	47976	47982	47989	47998
47970	47977	47985	47992	47999
47972	47978	47986	47994	
47974	47979	47987	47995	

Class 8F 2-8-0				
48007	48176	48201	48313	48387
48033	48178	48202	48324	48400
48037	48182	48203	48331	48418
48075	48187	48204	48350	48461
48112	48194	48205	48361	48463
48117	48196	48221	48362	48490
48133	48197	48273	48367	48553
48144	48199	48303	48370	48606
48168	48200	48304	48384	48607

48615	48637	48662	48685
48618	48638	48672	48690
48636	48655	48681	48694

Class 2F 0-6-0			
58146	58169	58176	58268
58153	58171	58192	58296
58159	58173	58197	

Total 155

Allocations: 1959 (18A)

Class 3P 4-4-2T
41947

Class 3F 0-6-0			
43251	43453	43650	43826
43309	43499	43793	43831

Class 4F 0-6-0			
43845	43990	44140	44224
43860	43994	44161	44284
43865	44012	44178	44376
43921	44106	44200	44427

Class 3F 0-6-0T		
47223	47247	47551

Class 8F 2-8-0				
48099	48185	48197	48306	48338
48118	48186	48201	48314	48350
48128	48187	48221	48319	48361
48145	48194	48271	48324	48362
48183	48195	48284	48332	48363
48184	48196	48304	48333	48367

48370	48517	48606	48636	48681
48384	48530	48607	48637	48685
48387	48538	48615	48640	48694
48490	48545	48616	48662	48698
48507	48604	48620	48672	48728

Class 2F 0-6-0

58153	58166	58173

Class 9F 2-10-0

92050	92078	92129	92153
92057	92086	92130	92156
92077	92094	92131	92158

Total 98

Allocations: 1965 (16A)

Class 8F 2-8-0

48056	48167	48193	48314	48681

Class 2MT 2-6-0

78042	78044	78055

Total 8

18B WESTHOUSES

Pre-Grouping Origin: Midland Railway
Gazetteer Ref: 41 D3
Closed: 1966
Shed-Codes: 18B (1948-1963)
16G (1963-1966)

Allocations: 1950 (18B)

Class 3F 0-6-0

43235	43254	43317	43379
43253	43266	43331	43580

Class 4F 0-6-0

43850	43880	43998	44191	44482
43860	43885	44014	44229	44605
43866	43966	44130	44321	
43867	43992	44188	44430	

Class 3F 0-6-0T
47466

Class 8F 2-8-0

48056	48118	48212	48494	48650
48057	48125	48280	48495	48661
48060	48136	48333	48534	48721
48063	48152	48353	48535	
48076	48184	48358	48589	
48083	48185	48391	48620	
48115	48186	48430	48623	

Class 2F 0-6-0

58166	58168	58196

Total 61

Allocations: 1959 (18B)

Class 3F 0-6-0

43235	43266	43825

Class 4F 0-6-0

43850	44130	44191	44285	44362
43866	44150	44229	44289	44430
43966	44173	44233	44321	44598

Class 3F 0-6-0T
47466

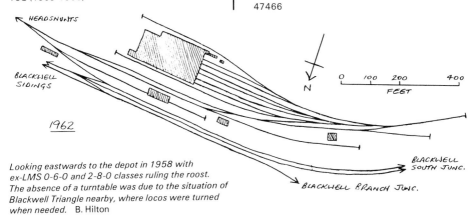

1962

Looking eastwards to the depot in 1958 with
ex-LMS 0-6-0 and 2-8-0 classes ruling the roost.
The absence of a turntable was due to the situation of
Blackwell Triangle nearby, where locos were turned
when needed.   B. Hilton

Class 8F 2-8-0
| 48057 | 48112 | 48204 | 48650 |
| 48060 | 48127 | 48353 | 48661 |

Class 9F 2-10-0
| 92113 | 92115 | 92117 |
| 92114 | 92116 | 92118 |

Total 33

Allocations: 1965 (16G)

Class 4F 0-6-0
43865	44118	44243	44420
43991	44203	44278	44528
44113	44218	44355

Class 3F 0-6-0T
| 47250 | 47535 | 47543 | 47611 |

Class 8F 2-8-0
48045	48145	48197	48384	48600
48046	48177	48204	48393	48620
48112	48184	48214	48432	48638
48127	48195	48258	48507	48750
48143	48196	48286	48538	48763

Class 9F 2-10-0
92153

Total 41

18C   HASLAND

Pre-Grouping Origin: Midland Railway
Gazetteer Ref: 41 C2
Closed: 1964
Shed-Codes: 18C (1948-1963)
16H (1963-1964)

Allocations: 1950 (18C)

Class 2P 4-4-0
| 40337 | 40409 | 40491 | 40537 | 40556 |
| 40359 | 40472 | 40503 | 40548 | 40557 |

Class OF 0-4-0ST
41518

Class OF 0-4-0T
| 41531 | 41532 |

Class 1F 0-6-0T
| 41813 | 41829 | 41874 |

Class 3F 0-6-0
| 43211 | 43219 | 43771 |
| 43212 | 43622 | 43802 |

Class 4F 0-6-0
43856	44054	44244	44294
43936	44107	44274	44410
43959	44162	44288

Class 0-4-0ST
| 47003 | 47004 |

Class 3F 0-6-0T
| 47272 | 47278 | 47423 | 47535 |

Class Beyer-Garratt 2-6-6-2T
| 47968 | 47973 | 47983 | 47990 | 47993 |
| 47971 | 47980 | 47984 | 47992 | 47997 |

Total 49

Allocations: 1959 (18C)

Class 2P 4-4-0
40691

Class 4 2-6-4T
| 42111 | 42186 | 42373 | 42490 |

Class 4F 0-6-0
43967	44122	44217	44603
43997	44133	44244
44053	44136	44288
44054	44162	44410

1962

CHESTERFIELD MIDLAND STN.   CLAY CROSS STN.

A 1954 view of the roundhouse clearly showing the partially roofed structure through the entrance. Class 4F No 44410 can be seen on the left whilst its sister engines occupy the turntable radii. Hasland shed shared the allocation of Beyer-Garratt locos with Toton (18A) until their withdrawal in 1957. *Photomatic*

Class OF 0-4-OST
47003	47004

Class 3F 0-6-OT
47218	47272	47278	47423	47535

Class 8F 2-8-0
48065	48095	48205	48364	48527
48082	48116	48212	48371	48547
48089	48125	48359	48494	

Total 39

18D STAVELEY MIDLAND

Pre-Grouping Origin: Midland Railway
Gazetteer Ref: 41 B3
Closed: 1965
Shed-Codes: 18D (1948-1958)
41E (1958-1965)
Allocations: 1950 (18D)

Class OF 0-4-OT
41528	41529	41533	41534

Class 1F 0-6-OT
41708	41711	41752	41763	41803
41710	41749	41753	41777	41804

Class 3F 0-6-0
43224	43292	43299	43386	43546
43234	43294	43309	43515	43575
43252	43298	43310	43524	43751

Class 4F 0-6-0
43857	43920	44070	44147	44590
43862	43993	44104	44154	
43886	44006	44122	44182	
43914	44066	44129	44299	

Class 3F 0-6-OT
47263	47426	47502	47626
47424	47455	47625	

Class 8F 2-8-0
48002	48210	48346	48538	48604
48053	48213	48441	48539	48663
48111	48332	48460	48545	
48195	48341	48493	48546	

Total 71

Allocations; 1959 (41E)

Class OF 0-4-OT
41528	41529	41531	41533

Class 1F 0-6-OT
41708	41739	41769
41734	41763	41804

The approaches to Staveley shed in 1957 with Class 3F No 43515 of the depot, heading a line of locos. The depot, also known as Barrow Hill, supplied a number of engines to the Staveley Iron & Chemical Company for shunting work, and the 0-4-OT class allocated were chosen mainly for their short wheelbase. As the shed-codes infer the depot came under the Eastern Region's control in 1958.
W. Potter

Class 3F 0-6-0

| 43234 | 43515 | 43711 | 43828 |
| 43386 | 43605 | 43729 | |

Class 4F 0-6-0

43863	44010	44129	44371	44606
43869	44066	44147	44404	
43886	44070	44205	44475	
43900	44088	44249	44482	
43920	44104	44267	44590	

Class 3F 0-6-0T

47221	47426	47619	47626
47263	47455	47620	47630
47424	47545	47625	47637

Class 8F 2-8-0

48037	48200	48341	48539	48772
48103	48210	48346	48546	
48164	48213	48515	48618	
48199	48331	48533	48663	

Total 67

Allocations: 1965 (41E)

Class 0F 0-4-0T

| 41528 | 41533 |

Class 1F 0-6-0T

| 41708 | 41734 | 41763 | 41804 | 41835 |

Class 4MT 2-6-0

| 43062 | 43082 | 43089 | 43143 | 43159 |
| 43080 | 43084 | 43111 | 43153 | 43161 |

Class 0F 0-4-0ST

| 47001 | 47005 |

Class WD 2-8-0

90084	90190	90474	90529	90587
90085	90340	90491	90572	90730
90189	90368	90509	90573	

Total 33

An interior view of the roundhouse in 1938 showing a good cross section of classes to be found at any one time. Although officially known as 'Grimesthorpe', the depot was occasionally referred to as 'Brightside' for an obvious reason when viewing the diagram. Diesel shunters first infiltrated the depot in 1956 and contributed to the relatively early closure of the shed to steam. The shed came under the Eastern Region's control in 1958. Real Photos

19A SHEFFIELD GRIMESTHORPE

Pre-Grouping Origin: Midland Railway
Gazetteer Ref: 21 G3
Closed: 1961
Shed Codes: 19A (1948-1958)
41B (1958-1961)
Allocations: 1950 (19A)

Class 3P 4-4-0

| 40728 | 40729 |

Class 1F 0-6-0T

| 41660 | 41781 | 41857 |

Class 5MT 2-6-0

| 42797 | 42904 |

Class 4MT 2-6-0

| 43015 | 43037 | 43041 |
| 43032 | 43038 | 43042 |

Class 3F 0-6-0

43241	43595	43636	43715	43775
43334	43604	43661	43731	
43335	43605	43662	43749	
43463	43607	43683	43755	

Class 4F 0-6-0

43844	44284	44426	44556
44211	44285	44437	44568
44212	44334	44550	44573

Class 5MT 4-6-0

44802	44858	45074	45262
44827	44944	45128	45407
44845	45056	45225	

Class 2MT 2-6-0

| 46450 | 46451 |

Class 3F 0-6-0T

| 47235 | 47432 | 47548 | 47611 |
| 47236 | 47513 | 47563 | 47624 |

Class 8F 2-8-0

| 48116 | 48216 | 48284 | 48642 |
| 48179 | 48219 | 48314 | |

Class 2F 0-6-0

| 58139 | 58151 | 58175 | 58220 | 58232 |
| 58140 | 58165 | 58190 | 58225 | 58276 |

Total 80

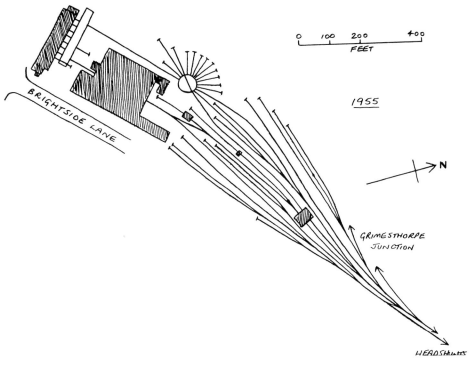

_1955_

BRIGHTSIDE LANE

GRIMESTHORPE JUNCTION

HEADSHUNTS

Allocations: 1959 (41B)

Class 1F 0-6-0T
41795   41857

Class 6P5F 2-6-0
42794   42797   42904

Class 3F 0-6-0
43174   43254   43406   43669   43751
43203   43307   43431   43715   43800
43222   43335   43634   43731
43243   43388   43637   43749

Class 4F 0-6-0
43844   44087   44287   44477   44573
43872   44174   44426   44535
43882   44212   44437   44547
44039   44265   44457   44568

Class 2 2-6-0
46450   46451

Class 3F 0-6-0T
47513   47548   47624   47636

Class 8F 2-8-0
48144   48179   48642
48178   48189   48765

Class 5 4-6-0
73000   73043   73074   73156

Total 56

19B MILLHOUSES

Pre-Grouping Origin: Midland Railway
Gazetteer Ref: 41 A2
Closed: 1962
Shed Codes: 19B (1948-1958)
41C (1958-1962)
Allocations: 1950 (19B)

Class 3MT 2-6-2T
40082   40139

Class 2P 4-4-0
40487   40493   40502   40518   40549

Class 4P 4-4-0
41014   41021   41062   41079
41016   41037   41072

Class 2MT 2-6-2T
41245   41246

Class 3F 0-6-0
43341

Class 5MT 4-6-0
44664   44962   44965   45264
44665   44963   44986   45297
44859   44964   45260

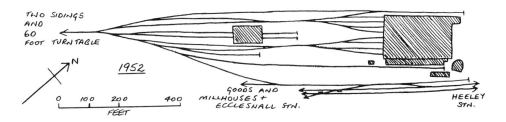

TWO SIDINGS AND 60 FOOT TURNTABLE

_1952_

GOODS AND MILLHOUSES + ECCLESHALL STN.

HEELEY STN.

A 1954 view of the ex-Midland depot with a
Class 2P 4-4-0 nearest the camera. Looking at the
right of the view, it would appear the shed was being
visited by enthusiasts. The shed transferred to the
Eastern Region in 1958. Photomatic

'Jubilee' 4-6-0
  45590 *Travancore*
  45594 *Bhopal*
  45607 *Fiji*
  45621 *Northern Rhodesia*
  45664 *Nelson*
  45679 *Armada*
  45683 *Hogue*
  45725 *Repulse*
Class 1P 0-4-4T
  58067   58068   58071   58076
Class 2F 0-6-0
  58209

Total 41

Allocations: 1959 (41C)

Class 3 2-6-2T
  40148
Class 4P 4-4-0
  40907
Class 2 2-6-2T
  41209   41245   41246
Class 4 2-6-0
  43032
Class 'Jubilee' 4-6-0
  45570 *New Zealand*
  45576 *Bombay*
  45590 *Travancore*
  45594 *Bhopal*
  45602 *British Honduras*
  45607 *Fiji*
  45609 *Gilbert and Ellice Islands*
  45654 *Hood*
  45656 *Cochrane*
  45664 *Nelson*
  45683 *Hogue*
  45725 *Repulse*
Class 2 2-6-0
  46400   46494
Class 5 4-6-0
  73004   73016   73048   73067   73155
  73011   73046   73065   73073
Class 2 2-6-0
  78022   78023   78024   78025

Total 33

19C CANKLOW

Pre-Grouping Origin: Midland Railway
Gazetteer Ref: 42 F1
Closed: 1965
Shed-Codes: 19C (1948-1958)
41D (1958-1965)
Allocations: 1950 (19C)

Class 3P 4-4-0
  40726
Class 1F 0-6-0T
  41797   41805   41835
Class 3F 0-6-0
  43180   43243   43660   43747
  43181   43325   43664   43814
  43208   43587   43669
Class 4F 0-6-0
  43906   44036   44127   44241   44576
  43950   44071   44128   44290
  44013   44089   44173   44457
  44015   44111   44232   44477
Class 3F 0-6-0T
  47546   47547
Class 8F 2-8-0
  48026   48065   48209   48434   48548
  48055   48140   48407   48450   48646
Class 2F 0-6-0
  58114   58147   58198   58233   58244
  58127   58170   58204   58238

Total 53

Allocations: 1959 (41D)

Class 1F 0-6-0T
  41835   41875
Class 4 2-6-0
  43037
Class 3F 0-6-0
  43225   43369   43395   43664   43814
  43361   43371   43660   43753
Class 4F 0-6-0
  44002   44071   44111   44245
  44036   44082   44128   44576
  44037   44089   44206
Class 8F 2-8-0
  48011   48138   48151   48209   48396
  48026   48140   48176   48216   48397
  48075   48150   48181   48391   48407

96

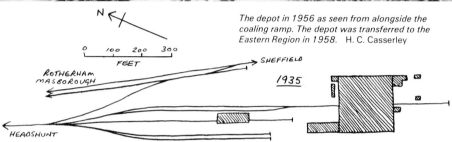

The depot in 1956 as seen from alongside the coaling ramp. The depot was transferred to the Eastern Region in 1958. H. C. Casserley

SHEFFIELD

ROTHERHAM MASBOROUGH

1935

HEADSHUNT

0   100   200   300
FEET

48508
Class 2F 0-6-0
58146   58170   58198
Class 5 4-6-0
73002
Class 2 2-6-0
78026   78027

Total 45

Allocations: 1965 (41D)

Class 4MT 2-6-0
43064   43091   43108   43109   43149
Class BI 4-6-0
61094   61313   61372   61394
61190   61315   61392
Class WD 2-8-0
90139   90203   90290   90410   90558
90149   90211   90330   90471   90658
90153   90220   90384   90557   90697

Total 27

20A   LEEDS HOLBECK

Pre-Grouping Origin: Midland Railway
Gazetteer Ref: 42 A3
Closed: 1967
Shed-Codes: 20A (1948-1957)
55A (1957-1967)
Allocations: 1950 (20A)

Class 3MT 2-6-2T
40075   40090   40169

Class 2P 4-4-0
40323   40326   40351   40362   40514
Class 3P 4-4-0
40743   40747   40758
Class 4P 4-4-0
41040   41048   41068   41137   41144
Class 2MT 2-6-2T
41267
Class 1F 0-6-0T
41745
Class 5MT 2-6-0
42795   42798   42816
Class 4MT 2-6-0
43016   43030   43039
Class 3F 0-6-0
43665
Class 4F 0-6-0
43931   44044   44404   44501
43953   44207   44431   44584
Class 5MT 4-6-0
44662   44757   44843   44856   45272
44753   44774   44849   44857
44754   44775   44850   44943
44755   44821   44853   44983
44756   44828   44854   45040
'Jubilee' 4-6-0
45562 *Alberta*
45565 *Victoria*
45566 *Queensland*
45568 *Western Australia*
45569 *Tasmania*
45573 *Newfoundland*
45587 *Baroda*
45589 *Gwalior*
45597 *Barbados*
45604 *Ceylon*
45605 *Cyprus*

A westerly view of the twin roundhouse from engine shed junction in LMS days. The shed became North Eastern property in 1957.
Crown Copyright National Railway Museum

WHITEHALL JUNC.

ENGINE SHED JUNC.

NINEVEH ROAD

N

1932

0   100   200   400
FEET.

'Jubilee' 4-6-0 continued
  45608 *Gibraltar*
  45619 *Nigeria*
  45626 *Seychelles*
  45651 *Shovell*
  45658 *Keyes*
  45659 *Drake*
  45675 *Hardy*
  45694 *Bellerophon*
  45739 *Ulster*
'Royal Scot' 4-6-0
  46103 *Royal Scots Fusilier*
  46108 *Seaforth Highlander*
  46109 *Royal Engineer*
  46117 *Welsh Guardsman*
  46133 *The Green Howards*
Class 3F 0-6-0T
  47254   47418   47420
Class 8F 2-8-0
  48067   48126   48159   48454
  48070   48157   48283   48537
  48104   48158   48399
Class 2P 2-4-2T
  50622
Class 1P 0-4-4T
  58060

Total 95

Allocations: 1959 (55A)

Class 3 2-6-2T
  40140   40193
Class 2P 4-4-0
  40491   40552   40690
Class 2 2-6-2T
  41267
Class 4 2-6-4T
  42052   42138
Class 6P5F 2-6-0
  42771   42774   42795   42798

Class 4 2-6-0
  43039   43055   43117   43130
  43043   43056   43124
Class 5 4-6-0
  44662   44756   44849   44857   45428
  44753   44757   44852   44943
  44754   44826   44853   44983
  44755   44828   44854   45273
'Jubilee' 4-6-0
  45562 *Alberta*
  45564 *New South Wales*
  45565 *Victoria*
  45566 *Queensland*
  45568 *Western Australia*
  45569 *Tasmania*
  45573 *Newfoundland*
  45589 *Gwalior*
  45597 *Barbados*
  45605 *Cyprus*
  45608 *Gibraltar*
  45619 *Nigeria*
  45639 *Raleigh*
  45658 *Keyes*

98

45659 *Drake*
45675 *Hardy*
45694 *Bellerophon*
45739 *Ulster*
'Royal Scot' 4-6-0
46109 *Royal Engineer*
46112 *Sherwood Forester*
46113 *Cameronian*
46117 *Welsh Guardsman*
46145 *The Duke of Wellington's Regiment*
    (West Riding)
Class 2 2-6-0
  46453   46493   46498
Class 3F 0-6-0T
  47420
Class 8F 2-8-0
  48067   48157   48159   48399   48454
  48104   48158   48283   48443
'Britannia' 4-6-2
  70044 *Earl Haig*
  70053 *Moray Firth*
  70054 *Dornoch Firth*
Class 5 4-6-0
  73010   73053   73069
  73045   73066   73171

                    Total 81

Allocations: 1965 (55A)

Class 4MT 2-6-4T
  42052   42139   42145   42271   42394
Class 4MT 2-6-0
  43039   43117   43124   43130
Class 5MT 4-6-0
  44662   44852   44857   45075   45211
  44824   44853   44983   45079   45273
  44828   44854   45063   45204
'Jubilee' 4-6-0
  45573 *Newfoundland*
  45593 *Kholapur*
  45608 *Gibraltar*
  45626 *Seychelles*
  45658 *Keyes*
  45660 *Rooke*
  45661 *Vernon*
  45664 *Nelson*
  45675 *Hardy*
  45697 *Achilles*
Class 8F 2-8-0
  48104   48158   48399   48542
  48157   48283   48454

                    Total 40

20B STOURTON

Pre-Grouping Origin: Midland Railway
Gazetteer Ref: 42 B2
Closed: 1967
Shed-Codes: 20B (1948-1957)
55B (1957-1967)
Allocations: 1950 (20B)

Class 1F 0-6-0T
  41666   41794   41859   41890
  41739   41838   41869
Class 3F 0-6-0
  43267   43456   43678   43737
  43392   43476   43681   43781
  43449   43579   43705
Class 4F 0-6-0
  43851   43878   43989   44153
  43852   43963   44020   44245
  43871   43987   44094   44467
Class 3F 0-6-0T
  47249   47443   47538   47640
  47271   47463   47589
Class 8F 2-8-0
  48123   48277   48622   48652
  48276   48311   48641   48703
Class 2F 0-6-0
  58136   58212   58245

                    Total 48

Allocations: 1959 (55B)

Class 4 2-6-0
  43014   43038   43044
Class 3F 0-6-0
  43456   43681   43737
Class 4F 0-6-0
  43871   44028   44207   44467
  43931   44044   44238   44570
  43968   44094   44335   44584
  43987   44153   44368   44586
Class 8F 2-8-0
  48055   48126   48311   48622   48703
  48076   48160   48352   48641   48721
  48084   48276   48358   48652

                    Total 36

Allocations: 1965 (55B)

Class 4MT 2-6-0
  43044   43135

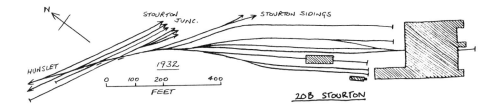

20B STOURTON

Looking towards the depot in 1952 showing the partially rebuilt shed of 1950. The depot was transferred to the North Eastern Region in 1957. W. Potter

Class 4F 0-6-0
| 44003 | 44028 | 44044 | 44570 |

Class 8F 2-8-0
48084	48130	48274	48473	48689
48093	48146	48311	48622	48703
48126	48160	48394	48641	48721

Class 3MT 2-6-0
| 77000 | 77003 | 77010 | 77013 |

Total 25

20C ROYSTON

Pre-Grouping Origin: LMS (1932)
Gazetteer Ref: 42 D2
Closed: 1967
Shed-Codes: 20C (1948-1957)
55D (1957-1967)
Allocations: 1950 (20C)

Class 3MT 2-6-2T
| 40074 | 40147 | 40181 | 40193 |

Class 2P 4-4-0
| 40444 | 40521 |

Class 4MT 2-6-4T
| 42142 | 42143 | 42145 |

Class 3F 0-6-0
| 43233 | 43332 | 43553 | 43789 |
| 43250 | 43446 | 43765 | |

Class 4F 0-6-0
| 43942 | 44003 | 44141 | 44161 | 44446 |

Class 3F 0-6-0T
| 47421 | 47448 | 47462 | 47581 | 47634 |

Class 8F 2-8-0
48062	48095	48169	48412	48443
48078	48103	48337	48419	48532
48080	48113	48376	48431	48540
48093	48162	48377	48439	48542

Class 3F 0-6-0
| 52095 | 52108 | 52252 | 52258 | 52559 |

Class 1P 0-4-4T
| 58052 | 58066 | 58075 | 58090 |

Class 2F 0-6-0
| 58156 | 58188 | 58237 | 58260 | 58265 |

Total 60

Looking north to the depot in 1953. Upon the closure of Cudworth (53E) in 1951, Royston received the six O4 class locos along with their crews and turns. Later in the same year the engines were exchanged for six of Colwick's (38A) WD 2-8-Os. The depot was transferred to the North Eastern Region in 1957. Photomatic

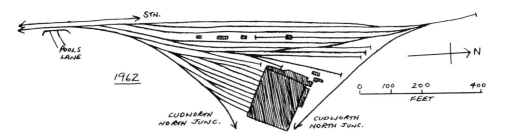

STN.

POOLS LANE

1962

CUDWORTH NORTH JUNC.

CUDWORTH NORTH JUNC.

N

0   100   200   400

FEET

20D NORMANTON

Allocations: 1959 (55D)

Class 3 2-6-2T
40082   40181
Class 2P 4-4-0
40581
Class 2 2-6-2T
41274   41281   41282
Class 3F 0-6-0
43233   43250   43267   43446   43789
Class 4F 0-6-0
43906   43983   44141   44446
43914   44003   44274   44550
43942   44107   44290   44582
Class 8F 2-8-0
48070   48130   48281   48473   48608
48078   48146   48337   48532   48664
48093   48162   48439   48537   48670
48113   48169   48466   48540   48689
48123   48222   48469   48542   48710
Class 2F 0-6-0
58191   58197   58260
Class 2 2-6-2T
84009
Class WD 2-8-0
90488   90611   90661

Total 55

Allocations: 1965 (55D)

Class 4F 0-6-0
43906   43968   43983   44056   44446
44912   45207   45219
Class 5MT 4-6-0
Class 8F 2-8-0
48067   48123   48222   48439   48540
48070   48159   48281   48443   48670
48075   48162   48337   48466   48710
48113   48169   48352   48537
Class WD 2-8-0
90377   90503   90605   90645   90650

Total 32

Pre-Grouping Origin: Lancashire & Yorkshire Railway
Gazetteer Ref: 42 C2
Closed: 1967
Shed Codes: 20D (1948-1957)
55E (1957-1967)
Allocations: 1950 (20D)

Class 3MT 2-6-2T
40179
Class 2P 4-4-0
40406   40480   40630
Class 1F 0-6-0T
41793   41844
Class 3F 0-6-0
43301   43509   43639   43714
43497   43514   43656
Class 4F 0-6-0
44098   44217   44338   44603
44099   44336   44562   44604
44151   44337   44586
Class 3F 0-6-0T
47239   47334   47335   47405
Class 8F 2-8-0
48084   48160   48274   48395   48547
48130   48164   48352   48396   48670
48131   48266   48357   48507   48702
48146   48271   48394   48508

Although originally of LYR building, the depot became the home of mainly ex-MR stock after 1927 when the ex-LYR engines moved on. This 1936 view shows a visiting LNER K3 class alongside the usual allocation of Midland 0-6-0s. In 1957, the shed found itself under the control of the North Eastern Region. LGRP courtesy David & Charles

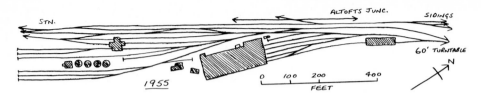

1955

Class 2P 2-4-2T
50621
Class 3F 0-6-0
52089

Total 49

Allocations: 1959 (55E)

Class 3 2-6-2T
40075   40179
Class 2P 4-4-0
40630
Class 4 2-6-0
43074   43114   43116
Class 3F 0-6-0
43183   43449   43639
43321   43509   43714
Class 4F 0-6-0
44098   44170   44337   44408   44604
44099   44336   44338   44458
Class J72 0-6-0T
68681   68701   68726
Class 5 4-6-0
73160   73161
Class WD 2-8-0
90012   90309   90362   90617   90673
90021   90337   90487   90637   90682
90247   90357   90610   90652   90722

Total 41

Allocations: 1965 (55E)

Class 4MT 2-6-4T
42083   42149
Class 4MT 2-6-0
43043   43116
Class 4F 0-6-0
44170   44400   44408   44458
Class WD 2-8-0
90243   90337   90395   90664   90722
90254   90345   90617   90682
90318   90357   90652   90699

Total 21

20E   BRADFORD MANNINGHAM

Pre-Grouping Origin: Midland Railway
Gazetteer Ref: 42A4
Closed: 1967
Shed Codes: 20E (1948-1957)
55F (1957-1967)
Allocations: 1950 (20E)

Class 3MT 2-6-2T
40069
Class 2P 4-4-0
40455   40489   40562   40567
Class 4P 4-4-0
41004   41067   41069   41080   41197
Class 2MT 2-6-2T
41265   41266
Class 4MT 2-6-4T
42146   42377   42380   42682   42685
Class 5MT 2-6-0
42762
Class 3F 0-6-0
43178   43351   43742   43770
Class 4F 0-6-0
44216   44400   44555   44570
Class 2MT 2-6-0
46452   46453
Class 3F 0-6-0T
47222   47255   47419

Looking north towards the shed in 1967, the last year of steam working. The depot was transferred to the North Eastern Region's control in 1957. W. Potter

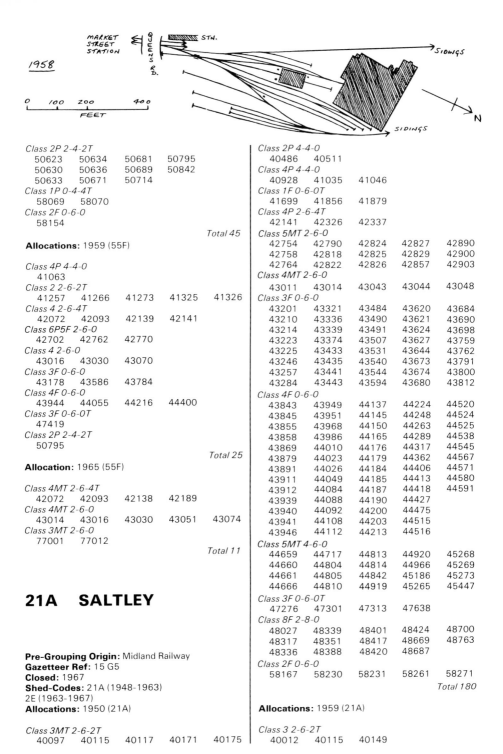

1958

FEET
0 100 200 400

MARKET STREET STATION
QUEENS RD.
STN.
SIDINGS
SIDINGS
N

Class 2P 2-4-2T
50623	50634	50681	50795
50630	50636	50689	50842
50633	50671	50714	

Class 1P 0-4-4T
58069 58070

Class 2F 0-6-0
58154

Total 45

Allocations: 1959 (55F)

Class 4P 4-4-0
41063

Class 2 2-6-2T
41257	41266	41273	41325	41326

Class 4 2-6-4T
42072	42093	42139	42141

Class 6P5F 2-6-0
42702 42762 42770

Class 4 2-6-0
43016 43030 43070

Class 3F 0-6-0
43178 43586 43784

Class 4F 0-6-0
43944 44055 44216 44400

Class 3F 0-6-0T
47419

Class 2P 2-4-2T
50795

Total 25

Allocation: 1965 (55F)

Class 4MT 2-6-4T
42072 42093 42138 42189

Class 4MT 2-6-0
43014 43016 43030 43051 43074

Class 3MT 2-6-0
77001 77012

Total 11

21A   SALTLEY

Pre-Grouping Origin: Midland Railway
Gazetteer Ref: 15 G5
Closed: 1967
Shed-Codes: 21A (1948-1963)
2E (1963-1967)
Allocations: 1950 (21A)

Class 3MT 2-6-2T
40097	40115	40117	40171	40175

Class 2P 4-4-0
40486 40511

Class 4P 4-4-0
40928 41035 41046

Class 1F 0-6-0T
41699 41856 41879

Class 4P 2-6-4T
42141 42326 42337

Class 5MT 2-6-0
42754	42790	42824	42827	42890
42758	42818	42825	42829	42900
42764	42822	42826	42857	42903

Class 4MT 2-6-0
43011	43014	43043	43044	43048

Class 3F 0-6-0
43201	43321	43484	43620	43684
43210	43336	43490	43621	43690
43214	43339	43491	43624	43698
43223	43374	43507	43627	43759
43225	43433	43531	43644	43762
43246	43435	43540	43673	43791
43257	43441	43544	43674	43800
43284	43443	43594	43680	43812

Class 4F 0-6-0
43843	43949	44137	44224	44520
43845	43951	44145	44248	44524
43855	43968	44150	44263	44525
43858	43986	44165	44289	44538
43869	44010	44176	44317	44545
43879	44023	44179	44362	44567
43891	44026	44184	44406	44571
43911	44049	44185	44413	44580
43912	44084	44187	44418	44591
43939	44088	44190	44427	
43940	44092	44200	44475	
43941	44108	44203	44515	
43946	44112	44213	44516	

Class 5MT 4-6-0
44659	44717	44813	44920	45268
44660	44804	44814	44966	45269
44661	44805	44842	45186	45273
44666	44810	44919	45265	45447

Class 3F 0-6-0T
47276 47301 47313 47638

Class 8F 2-8-0
48027	48339	48401	48424	48700
48317	48351	48417	48669	48763
48336	48388	48420	48687	

Class 2F 0-6-0
58167 58230 58231 58261 58271

Total 180

Allocations: 1959 (21A)

Class 3 2-6-2T
40012 40115 40149

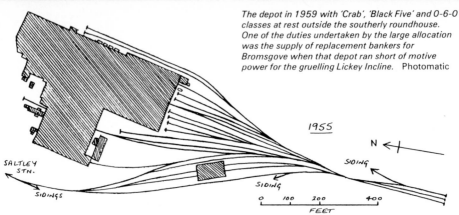

The depot in 1959 with 'Crab', 'Black Five' and 0-6-0 classes at rest outside the southerly roundhouse. One of the duties undertaken by the large allocation was the supply of replacement bankers for Bromsgove when that depot ran short of motive power for the gruelling Lickey Incline.   Photomatic

1955

Class 2P 4-4-0				
40443	40511			

Class 4 2-6-4T				
42054	42327	42337	42340	42383

Class 6P5F 2-6-0				
42758	42788	42813	42827	42890
42761	42790	42816	42846	42900
42775	42791	42823	42857	42903

Class 4 2-6-0			
43010	43017	43041	43047
43013	43036	43046	43049

Class 3F 0-6-0				
43210	43284	43433	43507	43673
43214	43339	43435	43594	43674
43219	43355	43468	43599	43680
43223	43374	43482	43620	43693
43242	43379	43484	43627	43812
43253	43381	43490	43644	

Class 4F 0-6-0			
43858	43986	44165	44230
43878	44004	44171	44263
43911	44013	44179	44333
43932	44026	44184	44406
43938	44084	44185	44413
43939	44091	44187	44463
43940	44092	44201	44515
43949	44108	44203	44520
43951	44137	44211	44580
43963	44138	44213	44583
43965	44143	44226	
43985	44160	44227	

Class 5 4-6-0				
44659	44804	44859	44963	45265
44660	44805	44888	44964	45268
44664	44813	44919	44965	45269
44666	44814	44920	44966	45272
44775	44841	44945	45040	45280
44776	44842	44962	45186	45333

Class 8F 2-8-0				
48002	48220	48339	48388	48669
48101	48315	48342	48523	48687
48105	48336	48351	48647	48700

Class 2F 0-6-0	
58168	58261

Class 9F 2-10-0				
92008	92051	92136	92150	92157
92009	92053	92137	92151	92165
92048	92120	92138	92152	92167
92049	92135	92139	92155	

Total 174

Allocations: 1965 (2E)

Class 5MT 4-6-0				
44663	44777	44910	44966	45280
44666	44829	44944	44981	45369
44775	44843	44945	45180	45410
44776	44873	44965	45264	45447

Class 2MT 2-6-0			
46443	46448	46454	46526

Class 8F 2-8-0				
48085	48109	48133	48220	48339

48351   48629   48646   48669
Class 4MT 2-6-0
76038   76043   76048   76052
Class 9F 2-10-0
92029   92136   92139   92152
92125   92137   92150   92155
92135   92138   92151   92164

Total 49

21B   BOURNVILLE

Pre-Grouping Origin: Midland Railway
Gazetteer Ref: 9 A4
Closed: 1960
Shed-Code: 21B (1948-1960)
Allocations: 1950

Class 3MT 2-6-2T
40105   40168
Class 2P 4-4-0
40439   40463
Class 4P 4-4-0
40917   41061   41064   41073
Class 4MT 2-6-4T
42050   42186   42327   42338   42342

Class 3F 0-6-0
43203   43355   43583   43675
43263   43359   43668   43687
Class 4F 0-6-0
44138   44333   44366
Class 5MT 4-6-0
44811   44852   45236   45274
Class 2F 0-6-0
58126   58138   58143

Total 31

Allocations: 1959

Class 3 2-6-2T
40144
Class 2P 4-4-0
40439   40568
Class 4 2-6-0
43012   43027   43033   43040
Class 3F 0-6-0
43263   43521   43583   43675
43359   43523   43668   43687
Class 4F 0-6-0
43855   44516   44571
Class 5 4-6-0
44981
Class 2F 0-6-0
58138   58143   58167

Total 22

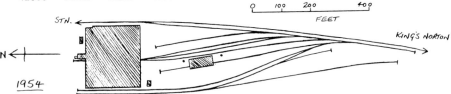

A 1958 view of the interior showing 4P, 4F, 5 and 3F clases around the turntable. Although the depot did not close until 1960, by 1959 Saltley (21A) had taken over most of its duties. Photomatic

A 1956 view showing two Class 3F 0-6-0 locos outside the depot; the southern end of the station can be seen on the left of the view. Bromsgrove, home of the famous 0-10-0 banking engine No 58100 ('Big Bertha') supplied additional power for trains ascending the nearby Lickey Incline. No 58100 was withdrawn in 1956. In 1958 the depot transferred from the LM Region to the Western, becoming 85F. Real Photos

21C   BROMSGROVE

Pre-Grouping Origin: Midland Railway
Gazetteer Ref: 9 A4
Closed: 1964
Shed-Codes: 21C (1948-1958)
85F (1958-1960)
85D (1961-1964)
Allocations: 1950 (21C)

Class 3F 0-6-0
  43667   43686
Class 3F 0-6-0T
  47234   47305   47425
  47303   47308   47565
Class 0-10-0
  58100
Beyer-Garratt 2-8-8-2T
  69999

Total 10

Allocations: 1959 (85F)

Class 94xx 0-6-0PT
  8400   8402   8404   8406
  8401   8403   8405
Class 3F 0-6-0
  43762
Class 3F 0-6-0T
  47276   47308
Class 9F 2-10-0
  92079

Total 11

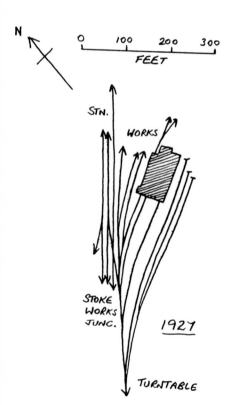

21D   STRATFORD-ON-AVON

Pre-Grouping Origin: Stratford-on-Avon &
Midland Junction Railway
Gazetteer Ref: 9 B5
Closed: 1957
Shed-Code: 21D (1948-1953)

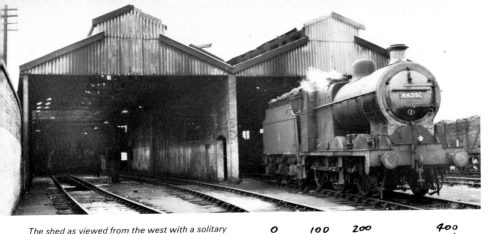

The shed as viewed from the west with a solitary 0-6-0 No 44391 on view in the year of closure. The building was demolished in the year of closure. W. Potter

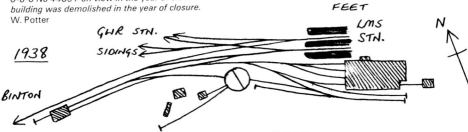

Allocation: 1950

Class 3F 0-6-0

43277	43520	43523	43693	43822
43381	43521	43568	43767	

Class 4F 0-6-0

43873	44186	44204	44587	44606

Total 14

In 1953 the shed lost its code and allocation and became a sub of Saltley (21A). The final allocation consisting of No 43520/68, 43873, 44043/186/242, 44524/67 were divided between Northampton (2E), Bedford (15D), Bourneville (21B) and Gloucester Barnwood (22B).

22A BRISTOL BARROW ROAD

Pre-Grouping Origin: Midland Railway
Gazetteer Ref: 3 A2
Closed: 1965
Shed-Codes: 22A (1948-1958)
82E (1958-1965)
Allocations: 1950 (22A)

Class 3MT 2-6-2T

40163	40164	40174

Class 2P 4-4-0

40423

Class 4P 4-4-0

40935	41028	41030

Class 1F 0-6-0T

41706

Class 4MT 2-6-0

43012	43046	43047

Class 3F 0-6-0

43427	43444	43464	43734
43436	43462	43712	

Class 4F 0-6-0

43847	43969	44267	44424	44537
43853	44135	44269	44466	44553
43926	44169	44335	44534	44569
43928	44266	44411	44536	

Class 5MT 4-6-0

44743	44745	44747
44744	44746	44855

'Jubilee' 4-6-0

45561 *Saskatchewan*
45570 *New Zealand*
45572 *Eire*
45660 *Rooke*
45662 *Kempenfelt*
45663 *Jervis*
45682 *Trafalgar*
45685 *Barfleur*
45690 *Leander*
45699 *Galatea*

Sentinel 0-4-0T

47190

Class 3F 0-6-0T

47544	47550	47678

Class 0F 0-4-0ST

51212

Total 58

A 1963 view of the shed yard taken from the Barrow Road overbridge. On display are BR Standard classes as well as 0-6-0 freight locos. In 1958 the depot came within the control of the Western Region. T. Nicholls

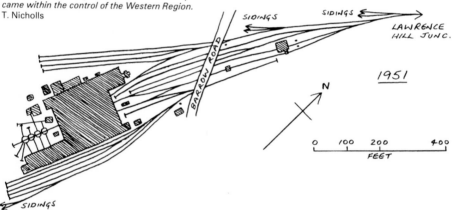

1951

Allocations: 1959 (82E)

Class 2251 0-6-0		
2215		
Class 43xx 2-6-0		
6346	6350	6376
Class 57xx 0-6-0PT		
8725		
Class 2P 4-4-0		
40332	40501	40537
Class 2 2-6-2T		
41207	41208	41240
Class 1F 0-6-0T		
41879		
Class 3F 0-6-0			
43344	43444	43593	43734
Class 4F 0-6-0			
43926	44411	44534	44553
44269	44424	44536	44569
44355	44466	44537	

'Patriot' 4-6-0				
45504 Royal Signals				
45506 The Royal Pioneer Corps				
45519 Lady Godiva				
'Jubilee' 4-6-0				
45572 Eire				
45577 Bengal				
45651 Shovell				
45660 Rooke				
45662 Kempenfelt				
45682 Trafalgar				
45685 Barfleur				
45690 Leander				
45699 Galatea				
Class 3F 0-6-0T				
47333	47544	47550	47552	47678
Class 0F 0-4-0ST				
51217	51221			
Class 5 4-6-0				
73003	73015	73054	73068	

Class 4 4-6-0
75004   75021   75022

Total 53

Allocations: 1965 (82E)

Class 57xx 0-6-0PT
3659	4684	9623	9680
3696	8714	9626	9711
4630	8795	9672	

Class 28xx 2-8-0
3802   3836   3863

'Hall' 4-6-0
4920 *Dumbleton Hall*
5932 *Haydon Hall*
6908 *Downham Hall*
6918 *Sandon Hall*

'Modified Hall' 4-6-0
6965 *Thirlestaine Hall*
6973 *Bricklehampton Hall*
6984 *Owsden Hall*
6990 *Witherslack Hall*
7907 *Hart Hall*
7914 *Lleweni Hall*
7924 *Thornycroft Hall*

'Grange' 4-6-0
6816 *Frankton Grange*
6829 *Burmington Grange*

Class 94xx 0-6-0PT
8403   8471   9405   9430

Class 4F 0-6-0
43924   44264   44269

Class 5MT 4-6-0
73003   73015   73030

Class 3MT 2-6-2T
82001   82036   82037   82038

Total 41

22B GLOUCESTER BARNWOOD

Pre-Grouping Origin: Midland Railway
Gazetteer Ref: 9 E3
Closed: 1964
Shed-Codes: 22B (1948-1958)
85E (1958-1960)
85C (1961-1964)
Allocations: 1950 (22B)

Class 3MT 2-6-2T
40040   40116

Class 2P 4-4-0
40523   40530

Class 4P 4-4-0
41001	41047	41074	41097
41025	41058	41078	

Class 0F 0-4-0T
41530   41537

Class 1F 0-6-0T
41720   41727

Class 3F 0-6-0
43213	43337	43373	43645
43258	43344	43506	43754

Class 4F 0-6-0
43846	43932	44045	44175
43887	43978	44087	44272
43924	44035	44167	

Class 3F 0-6-0T
47237   47607   47619   47620   47635

In 1950 Toton (18A) Beyer-Garratts began working in to Bristol with freight turns to Westerleigh sidings and Barrow Road depot had the job of turning them about for return journeys.

Looking west to the depot in LMS days past a line of Class 3F and 4F 0-6-0 locos. Along with its cohort (22A), Barnwood became part of the Western Region in 1958. IAL

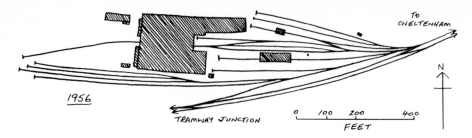

1956

TRAMWAY JUNCTION

0   100   200   400
        FEET

Class 1P 0-4-4T
  58034   58063
Class 2F 0-6-0
  58206

                      Total 42

Allocations: 1959 (85E)

Class 2P 4-4-0
  40489   40540
Class 4P 4-4-0
  41123
Class 0F 0-4-0T
  41535   41537
Class 2P 0-4-4T
  41900
Class 3F 0-6-0
  43337   43373   43520   43645   43754
Class 4F 0-6-0
  43853   44035   44167   44272
  43887   44045   44209   44296
  43924   44123   44264   44567
Class 2 2-6-0
  46401
Class 3F 0-6-0T
  47417   47422   47506   47539   47623
Class 4 4-6-0
  75009   75023

                      Total 31

Sheds 22C Bath, 22D Templecombe and 22E High-bridge have been catered for in the SR volume because of their SDJR origins and the fact that they spent the majority of their BR lifetimes in that Region as depots 71G, 71H and 71J respectively.

23A   SKIPTON

Pre-Grouping Origin: Midland Railway
Gazetteer Ref: 21 CI
Closed: 1967
Shed-Codes: 20F (1948-1950)
23A (1950-1951)
20F (1951-1957)
24G (1957-1963)
10G (1963-1967)
Allocations: 1950 (23A)

Class 2P 4-4-0
  40414   40422   40484
Class 1F 0-6-0T
  41767   41820   41855
Class 3P 4-4-2T
  41971   41972   41973   41974
Class 3F 0-6-0
  43295   43784
Class 4F 0-6-0
  43893   43917   43984   44007   44222
  43904   43944   43999   44041   44277
  43913   43960   44000   44197   44468
Class 2MT 2-6-0
  46440   46442
Class 3F 0-6-0T
  47427   47562
Class 8F 2-8-0
  48005   48145   48609

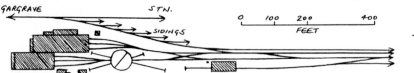

GARGRAVE   STN.

SIDINGS

0   100   200   400
        FEET

A Mid-1960s view of Skipton with Class 4MT 4-6-0 No 75059 nearest the camera. The roof was replaced in the 1950s. It will be noted that the depot's code was altered four times under the 19 years of ownership by BR.   N. Skinner

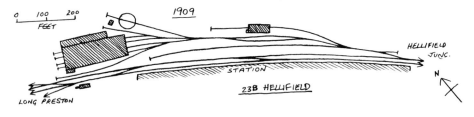

Class 1P 0-4-4T
58061   58077

Total 36

Allocations: 1959 (24G)

Class 2P 4-4-0
40586
Class 2 2-6-2T
41327
Class 4F 0-6-0
43893   43999   44041   44197   44277
43913   44000   44105   44220   44431
43960   44007   44119   44222   44468
Class 2 2-6-0
46442   46452
Class 3F 0-6-0T
47427   47428   47454
Class 4 2-6-0
76048
Class 2 2-6-2T
84015

Total 24

Allocations: 1965 (10G)

Class 4F 0-6-0
43893   43999   44063   44276   44277
Class 3F 0-6-0T
47201   47427   47602
Class 4MT 4-6-0
75011   75019   75042   75057
75015   75039   75044   75058
75017   75041   75051   75059
Class 2MT 2-6-2T
84015   84028

Total 22

Closed: 1963
Shed-Codes: 20G (1948-1950)
23B (1950-1951)
20G (1951-1957)
24H (1957-1963)
Allocations: 1950 (23B)

Class 3MT 2-6-2T
40021   40064   40162   40183   40184
Class 2P 4-4-0
40470
Class 2MT 2-6-2T
41205   41206
Class 5MT 2-6-0
42770   42784
Class 3F 0-6-0
43585   43586
Class 4F 0-6-0
44042   44149   44276   44282   44579
Class 8F 2-8-0
48105   48189   48608   48616
Class 2P 2-4-2T
50625   50686

Total 23

Allocations: 1959 (24H)

Class 2P 4-4-0
40685
Class 4 2-6-4T
42051   42278   42491   42648
42132   42484   42492
Class 3F 0-6-0
43585   43756
Class 4F 0-6-0
44149   44276   44282   44579
Class WD 2-8-0
90584

Total 15

23B   HELLIFIELD

Pre-Grouping Origin: Midland Railway
Gazetteer Ref: 24 C1

The depot in 1961 with WD 2-8-0 and 'Black Five'
classes sandwiching a 'Jubilee' loco No 45653
Barham. This view, taken from the station, shows the
boarded crossing which led from the platform to the
shed. In 1951 a small repair shop was built at the
depot.   Real Photos

23C LANCASTER

Pre-Grouping Origin: Midland Railway
Gazetteer Ref: 24 C3
Closed: 1966
Shed Codes: 20H (1948-1950)
23C (1950-1951)
11E (1951-1957)
24J (1957-1963)
10J (1963-1966)
Allocations: 1950 (23C)

Class 2P 4-4-0
40488
Class 4P 4-4-0
40931   41045   41065
41005   41056   41081
Class 2P 0-4-4T
41900   41901   41902   41904
Class 4MT 2-6-4T
42135   42136   42144
Class 5MT 2-6-0
42893   42895   42928
Class 4MT 2-6-0
43034   43035

Class 3F 0-6-0
43187   43293   43330
Class 4F 0-6-0
43890   44032   44280
43933   44201   44405
Class 2MT 2-6-0
46441
Class 3F 0-6-0T
47201   47468   47470   47532
47381   47469   47471   47639
Class 8F 2-8-0
48001   48148   48161

Total 40

Allocations: 1959 (24J)

Class 4P 4-4-0
41101
Class 2P 0-4-4T
41903   41904
Class 4 2-6-4T
42135   42136   42589
Class 6P5F 'Crab' 2-6-0
42810   42851   42893   42895   42928
Class 4 2-6-0
43018   43045   43113
43021   43112   43115
Class 3F 0-6-0
43257   43271   43295   43502

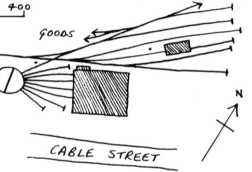

Looking east to the shed in 1960 with various classes of mixed traffic locos on view. By 1964 the depot had lost a lot of its duties to Carnforth (11A). This unusually laid out site often referred to as Green Ayre, had the distinction of being the only shed in the country to receive five different shed codes during BR days (20H, 23C, 11E, 24J and 10J).
Real Photos

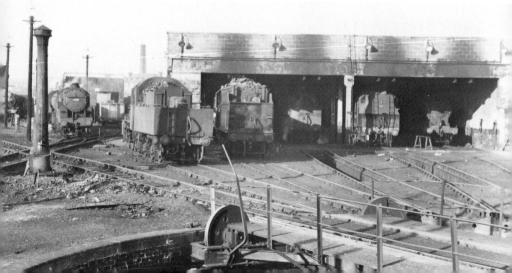

Class 2 2-6-0
46410   46426   46441
Class 3F 0-6-0T
47238   47468   47470   47532
47381   47469   47471   47639
Class 4 2-6-0
76084
Class WD 2-8-0
90595   90706

Total 35

Allocations: 1965 (10J)

Class 2MT 2-6-2T
41221   41251
Class 5MT 4-6-0
44667   44889   45025   45354   45394
44758   45014   45193   45373
Class 2MT 2-6-0
46422   46431   46433   46441
Class 8F 2-8-0
48148   48218   48297   48679

Total 19

24A   ACCRINGTON

Pre-Grouping Origin: Lancashire &
Yorkshire Railway
Gazetteer Ref: 24 E1

Closed: 1961
Shed-Code: 24A (1948-1961)
Allocations: 1950

Class 2P 4-4-0
40676   40677   40680   40681
Class 4P 4-4-0
41188
Class 4MT 2-6-4T
42153   42433   42548   42634   42661
42295   42437   42549   42643
Class 5MT 2-6-0
42716   42717   42718   42843
Class 4F 0-6-0
44460   44479   44486
Class 5MT 4-6-0
45367   45396
Class 2F 0-6-0ST
51410   51514
Class WD 2-8-0
90206   90416   90632
90402   90610   90713

Total 31

Allocations: 1959

Class 4 2-6-4T
42110   42294   42433   42619   42643
42153   42295   42480   42620   42661

1931

*Taken shortly after steam closure this 1961 view
shows the size of the depot having diminished to six
road status compared with the original eight road*
*building. Upon closure in 1961 the engines and men
went to Rose Grove (24B). The depot then
concentrated on the housing of dmus.*   W. T. Stubbs

Class 5 4-6-0
44689	44889	45078	45227
44692	45068	45226	45415

Class 3F 0-6-0T
47201	47562

Class WD 2-8-0
90374	90399

Total 22

24B ROSE GROVE

Pre-Grouping Origin: Lancashire & Yorkshire Railway
Gazetteer Ref: 24 D1
Closed: 1968
Shed-Codes: 24B (1948-1963)
10F (1963-1968)
Allocations: 1950 (24B)

Class 4MT 2-6-4T
42187	42475	42547
42438	42546	42555

Class 5MT 2-6-0
42706	42733	42821

Class 4F 0-6-0
44038	44221	44464	44544

Class 3F 0-6-0T
47386	47575	47576

Class 8F 2-8-0
48319	48435

Class 2P 2-4-2T
50653	50654

Class 2F 0-6-0ST
51336	51497

Class WD 2-8-0
90109	90183	90274	90399	90599
90122	90227	90283	90420	90621
90126	90231	90314	90557	90687
90138	90241	90348	90576	
90159	90258	90371	90584	
90171	90264	90387	90592	

Total 49

Allocations: 1959 (24B)

Class 4 2-6-4T
42187	42438	42474	42547
42280	42439	42546	42555

Class 6P5F 2-6-0
42706	42717	42869
42716	42828	42898

Class 5 4-6-0
44780	44948	45205	45229
44940	44949	45209	

Class 3F 0-6-0T
47386	47575	47576	47577	47586

Class 3F 0-6-0
52095	52179	52526

Class 2 2-6-2T
84010

Class WD 2-8-0
90109	90171	90241	90371
90138	90181	90264	90420
90143	90183	90274	90557
90159	90231	90314	90592

Total 46

A view of the shed yard taken in 1968 from the coaling plant showing the monopoly the Class 8 freight locos had in the final year of steam working.

The depot was one of the last three open to steam traction, closing in August 1968.
J. Bentley collection

Allocations: 1965 (10F)

Class 5MT 4-6-0

44894	45196	45210	45218
44940	45205	45216	45397

Class 3F 0-6-0T

47383	47631

Class WD 2-8-0

90040	90181	90295	90420	90681
90080	90207	90364	90448	90725
90171	90241	90367	90541	

Total 24

24C LOSTOCK HALL

Pre-Grouping Origin: Lancashire & Yorkshire
Railway
Gazetteer Ref: 24 E3
Closed: 1968
Shed-Codes: 24C (1948-1963)
10D (1963-1968)
Allocations: 1950 (24C)

Class 4MT 2-6-4T

42158	42434	42480	42492
42296	42435	42481	42556
42298	42436	42491	

Class 2P 2-4-2T

50852

Class 2F 0-6-0ST

51345	51423	51526

Class 3F 0-6-0

52160	52238	52336	52522
52171	52272	52368	52523
52216	52296	52399	52524
52220	52317	52456	52527

Class WD 2-8-0

90295	90331	90398	90640	90689
90320	90335	90541	90658	
90328	90367	90595	90681	

Total 44

Allocations: 1959 (24C)

Class 3 2-6-2T

40192

Class 4 2-6-4T

42158	42296	42434	42481
42286	42298	42476	42634

Class 3F 0-6-0

52182	52429	52456
52290	52445	52458

Class WD 2-8-0

90258	90331	90413	90675
90266	90335	90541	90681
90277	90367	90556	90689
90295	90398	90658	90720

Total 31

Allocation: 1965 (10D)

Class 4MT 2-6-4T

42081	42296	42436	42546
42187	42297	42442	42625

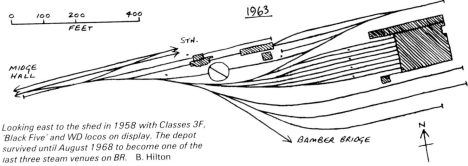

1963

0	100	200	400
FEET

MIDGE HALL

STN.

BAMBER BRIDGE

N

*Looking east to the shed in 1958 with Classes 3F,
'Black Five' and WD locos on display. The depot
survived until August 1968 to become one of the
last three steam venues on BR. B. Hilton*

115

Class 5MT 4-6-0
44816	45197	45226

Class 3F 0-6-0T
47293	47336	47454	47472

Class 8F 2-8-0
48039	48328	48419	48438	48707
48307	48400	48434	48470	48730

Class 2MT 2-6-0
78002	78037	78041
78022	78040	78057

Class WD 2-8-0
90125	90720

Total 33

24D LOWER DARWEN

Pre-Grouping Origin: Lancashire & Yorkshire
Railway
Gazetteer Ref: 24 E2
Closed: 1966
Shed-Codes: 24D (1948-1963)
10H (1963-1966)
Allocations: 1950 (24D)

Class 2P 4-4-0
40588

Class 4P 2-6-4T
42147	42180	42483	42485	42558
42154	42439	42484	42490	42559

Class 4F 0-6-0
43897	44240	44398
44225	44291	44483

Class 2F 0-6-0ST
51415	51499	51506

Class 3F 0-6-0
52203	52268	52431	52445	52529
52260	52289	52441	52460	52579
52262	52363	52444	52526	

Class WD 2-8-0
90178	90266	90357	90374

Total 38

Allocations: 1959 (24D)

Class 3 2-6-2T
40120	40162	40163	40183

Class 4 2-6-4T
42147	42483	42558
42154	42485	42559

Class 6P5F 2-6-0
42718	42722	42729	42796	42821

Class 4F 0-6-0
43897	44398	44460	44479	44483

Class 4 2-6-0
76080	76081	76082	76083

Class 2 2-6-2T
84011	84012

Total 26

Allocations: 1965 (10H)

Class 5MT 2-6-0
42727	42828	42892
42732	42869	42898

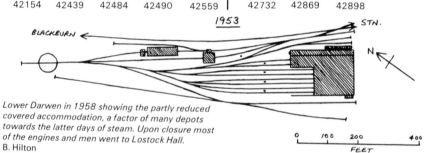

1953

BLACKBURN ←

STN.

N

Lower Darwen in 1958 showing the partly reduced
covered accommodation, a factor of many depots
towards the latter days of steam. Upon closure most
of the engines and men went to Lostock Hall.
B. Hilton

0   100   200   400
FEET

Class 4MT 2-6-0
43019   43041   43118   43119
Class WD 2-8-0
90148   90152   90187   90204   90261
Total 15

25A WAKEFIELD

Pre-Grouping Origin: Lancashire & Yorkshire
Railway
Gazetteer Ref: 21 E3
Closed: 1967
Shed-Codes: 25A (1948-1956)
56A (1956-1967)
Allocations: 1950 (25A)

Class 2MT 2-6-2T
41250   41251   41252   41253   41254
Class 5MT 4-6-0
45101   45205   45209   45261
45204   45206   45221   45339
Class 2MT 2-6-0
46438   46439
Class 3F 0-6-0T
47510   47572   47573   47580   47582
Class 8F 2-8-0
48502   48504   48506   48511   48514
Class 7F 0-8-0
49625
Class 2P 2-4-2T
50650   50715   50788   50873   50898
50656   50762   50799   50886
50712   50764   50869   50892
Class 2F 0-6-0ST
51447
Class 2F 0-6-0
52041   52043   52044
Class 3F 0-6-0
52120   52235   52345   52386   52561
52150   52284   52351   52433   52576
52154   52305   52353   52435
52186   52319   52369   52521
Class WD 2-8-0
90124   90339   90415   90652
90157   90341   90417   90654
90163   90342   90581   90656
90187   90353   90607   90667
90197   90361   90615   90673
90212   90362   90617   90679
90237   90363   90620   90682
90242   90370   90624   90692
90243   90379   90631   90710
90249   90380   90633   90719
90292   90381   90635   90722
90310   90396   90637   90725
90329   90397   90639   90729
90333   90404   90643
90334   90412   90644
90337   90414   90651

Total 122

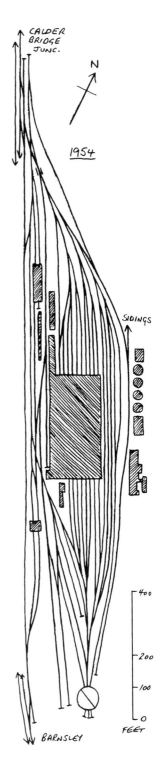

CALDER BRIDGE JUNC.

N

1954

SIDINGS

400

200

100

0

FEET

BARNSLEY

The north end of the depot in 1937. The depot became part of the North Eastern Region in 1956. W. Potter

Allocations: 1959 (56A)

Class 3 2-6-2T
| 40117 | 40139 | 40155 | 40169 |

Class 2 2-6-2T
| 41264 |

Class 6P5F 2-6-0
| 42861 | 42862 | 42863 |

Class 4F 0-6-0
| 44019 |

Class 2 2-6-0
| 46413 | 46435 | 46438 |

Class 3F 0-6-0T
| 47271 | 47510 | 47567 | 47572 | 47580 |
| 47463 | 47538 | 47571 | 47573 | 47582 |

Class 2F 0-6-0
| 52044 |

Class 3F 0-6-0
| 52133 | 52355 |

Class B1 4-6-0
| 61015 *Duiker* | 61131 | 61296 |
| 61017 *Bushbuck* | 61268 | 61385 |

Class O4 2-8-0
| 63588 | 63857 | 63864 | 63920 |

Class J50 0-6-0T
| 68904 | 68910 | 68939 |

Class WD 2-8-0
90016	90321	90379	90497	90639
90047	90326	90380	90581	90644
90056	90339	90382	90604	90651
90061	90341	90385	90607	90654
90076	90342	90396	90615	90656
90089	90348	90404	90620	90679
90100	90353	90414	90625	90692
90112	90361	90415	90631	90710
90116	90363	90417	90633	90719
90124	90370	90429	90635	

Total 87

Allocations: 1965 (56A)

Class 4MT 2-6-4T
42108	42161	42269
42150	42181	42406
42152	42204	42650

'Jubilee' 4-6-0
45565 *Victoria*
45694 *Bellerophon*
45739 *Ulster*

Class B1 4-6-0
61022 *Sassaby*	61123	61161	61320
61024 *Addax*	61129	61173	61353
61040 *Roedeer*	61131	61224	61387

Class WD 2-8-0
90054	90160	90342	90407	90622
90061	90200	90348	90415	90631
90068	90210	90360	90417	90633
90074	90233	90363	90429	90639
90076	90281	90370	90430	90651
90089	90300	90373	90457	90654
90112	90321	90379	90470	90678
90113	90329	90380	90482	90679
90116	90333	90382	90610	90684
90122	90336	90385	90611	90698
90124	90339	90396	90615	90707
90155	90341	90404	90620	90721

Total 84

As will be seen, the large allocation of ex-WD locos was maintained throughout the depot's BR lifetime. In 1956, No 52044 became the last ex-LYR Barton-Wright in service and remained so until its withdrawal in 1959. Thankfully the engine escaped the cutter's torch and was set aside for preservation.

25B   HUDDERSFIELD

Pre-Grouping Origin: LNWR
Gazetteer Ref: 21 E2
Closed: 1967
Shed-Codes: 25B (1948-1956)
55G (1957-1967)
Allocations: 1950 (25B)

Class 4MT 2-6-4T
| 42310 | 42312 | 42408 | 42410 | 42413 |
| 42311 | 42384 | 42409 | 42412 | 42414 |

Class 5MT 2-6-0
| 42861 | 42862 | 42863 | 42866 | 42869 |

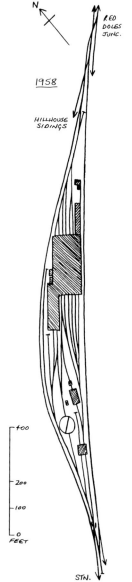

A northerly view of the depot in 1950. The shed, sometimes known as Hillhouse, transferred to the North Eastern Region's control in 1957. B. Hilton

N

RED DOLES JUNC.

1958

HILLHOUSE SIDINGS

400

200

100

0

FEET

STN.

Class 5MT 4-6-0
44780	44949	45215	45238
44824	45099	45237	45340

'Jubilee' 4-6-0
45596 *Bahamas*

Class 7F 0-8-0
49648

Class 2P 2-4-2T
50731	50735	50736	50887

Class 2F 0-6-0ST
51408	51524

Class WD 2-8-0
90181	90345	90619	90680
90308	90347	90650	90694
90332	90527	90655	

Total 42

Allocations: 1959 (55G)

Class 4 2-6-4T
42310	42377	42408	42410	42413
42312	42384	42409	42412	42414

Class 5 4-6-0
73162	73163	73164	73165	73166

Class WD 2-8-0
90243	90332	90619	90680
90249	90345	90621	90694
90325	90347	90624	

Total 26

Allocations: 1965 (55G)

Class 4MT 2-6-4T
42141	42317	42410	42618

Class WD 2-8-0
90325	90347	90619	90680
90332	90362	90649	90694

Total 12

The remains of Goole depot in 1950 depicting three of its allocation of Class 2F saddle tanks namely (left to right) Nos 51361, 51323 and 11516 (later renumbered 51516). The shed, situated in the heart of Goole's dockland was not easy to find for the average spotter. In 1956 the depot became North Eastern Region property. Real Photos

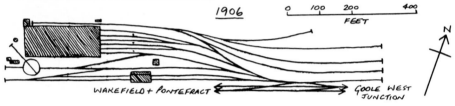

25C   GOOLE

Pre-Grouping Origin: Lancashire & Yorkshire Railway
Gazetteer Ref: 22 E5
Closed: 1967
Shed-Codes: 25C (1948-1956)
53E (1956-1960)
50D (1960-1967)
Allocations: 1950 (25C)

Class 2P 4-4-0
40586   40589   40685
Class 4MT 2-6-4T
42411
Class 4F 0-6-0
44062   44105   44220   44485
Class 2MT 2-6-0
46405   46407   46408   46409   46437
Class 8F 2-8-0
48449   48738   48768
Class OF 0-4-0ST
51207   51222   51241   51244
Class 2F 0-6-0ST
51323   51379   51516
51361   51432   51521
Class 2F 0-6-0
52037   52056
Class 3F 0-6-0
52133   52273   52592
Class WD 2-8-0
90228   90262   90281

Total 34

Allocations: 1959 (53E)

Class 1F 0-6-0T
41661   41797   41855

Class 4 2-6-4T
42436
Class 2 2-6-0
46407   46408   46409   46415
Class OF 0-4-0ST
51222   51241   51244
Class 3F 0-6-0
52154   52244   52252   52305   52319
Class WD 2-8-0
90094   90228   90265   90478
90186   90260   90281   90531
90213   90262   90300

Total 27

Allocations: 1965(50D)

Class 4MT 2-6-0
43098   43125
Class WD 2-8-0
90072   90094   90172   90427
90081   90099   90273   90451
90091   90132   90406

Total 13

25D   MIRFIELD

Pre-Grouping Origin: Lancashire & Yorkshire Railway
Gazetteer Ref: 21 E2
Closed: 1967
Shed-Codes: 25D (1948-1956)
56D (1956-1967)
Allocations: 1950 (25D)

Class 4MT 2-6-4T
42152   42405   42407
42324   42406   42553

120

The depot in 1957, a year after its transfer to the North Eastern Region. On display are Class 2 and 4 tanks, a WD 2-8-0 and Class 3F and 7F locos. Photomatic

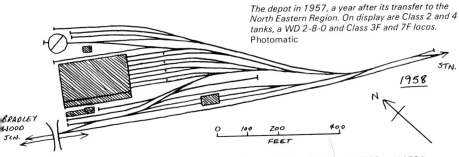

BRADLEY WOOD JCN.

1958

N

0   100   200   400
FEET

STN.

Class 5MT 2-6-0
42700   42712   42719
Class 4F 0-6-0
44056   44471   44474
Class 8F 2-8-0
48720   48751   48755
Class 7F 0-8-0
49598   49618   49659   49661   49663
49602   49620   49660   49662
Class 2F 0-6-0ST
51358   51453
Class 3F 0-6-0
52124   52191   52331   52408   52515
52166   52255   52388   52448
Class WD 2-8-0
90543   90578   90622   90642   90723
Total 40

Allocations: 1959 (56D)

Class 4 2-6-4T
42152   42285   42324   42406   42407
Class 3F 0-6-0
43705
Class 4F 0-6-0
44056   44474   44485
Class 3F 0-6-0T
47335
Class 8F 2-8-0
48202   48265   48274   48357
Class 2F 0-6-0ST
51358
Class 3F 0-6-0
52089   52121   52139   52515
Class B1 4-6-0
61011 *Waterbuck*
61040 *Roedeer*
Class WD 2-8-0
90126   90622   90642   90655   90678

90707   90721   90723   90731
Total 30

Allocations: 1965 (56D)

Class 5MT 4-6-0
44693   44695   44951   45208
44694   44946   44990
Class 8F 2-8-0
48055   48202   48276   48358
48138   48265   48357   48608
Class WD 2-8-0
90310   90351   90397   90655
Total 19

25E   SOWERBY BRIDGE

Pre-Grouping Origin: Lancashire & Yorkshire Railway
Gazetteer Ref: 21 El
Closed: 1964
Shed-Codes: 25E (1948-1956)
56E (1956-1964)
Allocations: 1950 (25E)

Class 4MT 2-6-4T
42149   42150   42151   42639
Class 3F 0-6-0T
47508   47509
Class 7F 0-8-0
49540
Classes 2P & 3P* 2-4-2T
50765   50925*
Class 2F 0-6-0ST
51348   51381   51479   51488   51503

121

Looking west towards the depot in 1954 shortly after the building was re-roofed by the LMR. In 1956 the shed came under the control of the North Eastern Region.   W. Potter

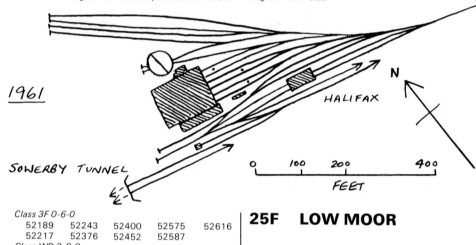

1961

SOWERBY TUNNEL

HALIFAX

N

FEET

0   100   200   400

Class 3F 0-6-0
52189	52243	52400	52575	52616
52217	52376	52452	52587	

Class WD 2-8-0
90277	90385	90531	90707	90728
90321	90406	90593	90724	90731

Total 33

Allocations: 1959(56E)

Class 3 2-6-2T
40147

Class 4 2-6-4T
42094	42150	42311	42405
42149	42151	42380	

Class 4 2-6-0
43126

Class 3F 0-6-0T
47266	47299	47379	47508	47509

Class 3F 0-6-0
52351	52400	52411	52452

Class WD 2-8-0
90113	90210	90329	90412
90122	90310	90360	90470

Total 26

25F   LOW MOOR

Pre-Grouping Origin: Lancashire & Yorkshire Railway
Gazetteer Ref: 21 E2
Closed: 1967
Shed-Codes: 25F (1948-1956)
56F (1956-1967)
Allocations: 1950 (25F)

Class 4MT 2-6-4T
42107	42110	42113	42116
42108	42111	42114	42188
42109	42112	42115	42189

Class 5MT 2-6-0
42726	42728	42828
42727	42732	42865

Class 5MT 4-6-0
44912	44990	45207
44951	45201	45208

Classes 2P/3P 2-4-2T
50806	50909

Class 2F 0-6-0ST
51404

122

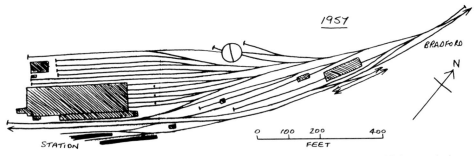

1957

STATION

BRADFORD

N

0   100   200   400
FEET

'Jubilee' 4-6-0 No 45581 Bihar and Orissa *on shed in 1966 a year before steam closure.*   I. G. Holt

Class 3F 0-6-0

52092	52237	52410	52427	52590
52104	52309	52411	52461	

Class 7F 0-8-0

52857

Total 37

Allocations: 1959 (56F)

Class 2 2-6-2T

41250	41253	41262	41263

Class 4 2-6-4T

42073	42108	42188	42622
42084	42109	42189	42649
42107	42116	42411	42650

Class 4 2-6-0

43100

Class 3F 0-6-0

43579

Class 4F 0-6-0

44062

Class 5 4-6-0

44693	44824	44951	45208
44694	44912	44990	45219
44695	44946	45207	

Class 2 2-6-0

46483

Class 3F 0-6-0T

47255	47405	47446	47635

Class 8F 2-8-0

48080	48394	48702

Class 3F 0-6-0

52413	52461

Class B1 4-6-0

61020 *Gemsbok*	61049
61023 *Hirola*	61230
61039 *Steinbok*	61383

Class J6 0-6-0

64170	64203	64226

Class J39 0-6-0

64791	64801	64872	64903	64919
64796	64817	64886	64907	

Class J50 0-6-0T

68895	68912	68923	68933	68944
68908	68922	68932	68943	68969

Class WD 2-8-0

90333   90711

Total 70

Allocations: 1965 (56F)

Class 4MT 2-6-4T

42055	42107	42116	42117	42664
42073	42109	42142	42285	

123

Class B1 4-6-0
  61023 *Hirola*
  61115
  61189 *Sir William Gray*
  61214
  61309
  61386
Class WD 2-8-0
  90711   90723

Total 17

The large 1959 allocation was a result of the closure to steam of the nearby Bradford Hammerton Street depot (37C) in 1958, when all of the men and locos were transferred to Low Moor which by this time was itself part of the Eastern network, albeit north.

25G FARNLEY
JUNCTION

Pre-Grouping Origin: LNWR
Gazetteer Ref: 21 D3
Closed: 1966
Shed-Codes: 25G (1948-1956)
55C (1956-1966)

Allocations: 1950 (25G)

Class 2MT 2-6-2T

41255	41256	41257	42158	41259

Class 5MT 2-6-0

42730	42731

Class 2MT 4-6-0

44896	45063	45076	45080	45341
45062	45075	45078	45218	

'Jubilee' 4-6-0
  45702 *Colossus*
  45704 *Leviathan*
  45705 *Seahorse*
  45708 *Resolution*
  45711 *Courageous*

Class 3F 0-6-0

47567	47568	47569	47570	47571

Class 8F 2-8-0
  48456

Class WD 2-8-0

90140	90322	90372	90645	90698
90204	90325	90395	90649	90699
90245	90326	90407	90664	90711
90316	90336	90588	90666	
90318	90351	90591	90684	

Total 50

Allocations: 1959 (55C)

Class 2P 4-4-0
  40584

CHURWELL

1963

LINES
MEET

N

STN.

FEET 0   100   200   400

The depot in 1952 looking from the east. Like all the '25' group of sheds, Farnley was transferred to the North Eastern Region's control in 1956.   W. Potter

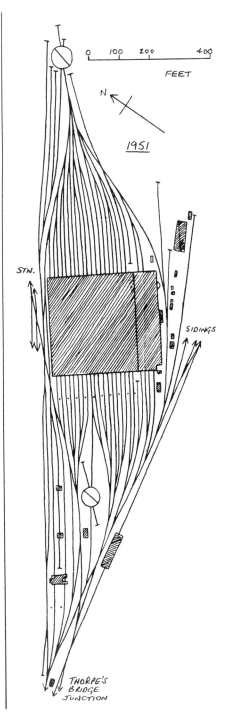

Class 2 2-6-2T
| 41254 | 41255 | 41256 | 41258 | 41259 |

Class 6P5F 2-6-0
| 47213 | 42766 | 42789 | 42865 | 42866 |

Class 5 4-6-0
| 44896 | 45075 | 45080 | 45211 |
| 45063 | 45079 | 45204 | |

'Jubilee' 4-6-0
45581 *Bihar & Orissa*
45646 *Napier*
45695 *Minotaur*
45708 *Resolution*

Class 3F 0-6-0T
| 47568 | 47569 | 47570 |

Class WD 2-8-0
90127	90334	90562	90650	90726
90254	90336	90588	90664	90728
90308	90351	90591	90666	
90318	90395	90645	90684	
90322	90407	90649	90699	

Total 47

Allocations: 1965 (55C)

Class 5MT 4-6-0
| 44826 | 44896 | 44943 | 45080 | 45428 |

'Jubilee' 4-6-0
45562 *Alberta*
45581 *Bihar & Orissa*
45643 *Rodney*
45647 *Sturdee*

Class 8F 2-8-0
| 48076 | 48080 | 48664 |

Total 12

26A NEWTON HEATH

Pre-Grouping Origin: Lancashire & Yorkshire Railway
Gazetteer Ref: 20 B1
Closed: 1968
Shed-Codes: 26A (1948-1963)
9D (1963-1968)
Allocations: 1950 (26A)

Class 3MT 2-6-2T
| 40013 | 40015 | 40063 | 40065 |

Class 4MT 2-6-4T
42278	42284	42290	42621	42630
42279	42285	42477	42622	42635
42280	42286	42486	42623	
42281	42287	42550	42624	
42282	42288	42551	42625	
42283	42289	42618	42626	

Class 5MT 2-6-0
42701	42707	42713	42789	42901
42702	42708	42714	42820	
42703	42709	42715	42845	
42704	42710	42750	42871	
42705	42711	42766	42878	

Class 4F 0-6-0
| 44311 | 44543 |

Class 5MT 4-6-0

44734	44893	45079	45210	45232
44735	44894	45102	45211	45233
44736	44895	45103	45219	45234
44888	44933	45104	45220	
44889	44934	45105	45222	
44890	44940	45202	45223	
44891	44987	45203	45224	

'Jubilee' 4-6-0
45635 *Tobago*
45642 *Boscawen*
45661 *Vernon*
45671 *Prince Rupert*
45700 *Britannia*
45701 *Conqueror*
45706 *Express*
45710 *Irresistible*
45712 *Victory*
45719 *Glorious*

Class 2MT 2-6-0
46418   46419

Class 3F 0-6-0T
47577   47586

Class 8F 2-8-0

48705	48719	48730	48752
48707	48722	48733	48754
48714	48726	48735	48761
48715	48727	48739	48769

Class 7F 0-8-0

49531	49558	49612	49657
49536	49560	49637	49673
49545	49580	49650	49674
49554	49608	49651	

Class 2P 2-4-2T
50855   50859

Class 2F 0-6-0ST

51338	51429	51458	51496
51424	51436	51470	51510
51425	51457	51472	

Class 3F 0-6-0

52094	52139	42266	52355	52558
52102	52156	52300	52358	52569
52132	52207	52304	52455	52583
52137	52239	52343	52517	

Class B1 4-6-0
61326

Class WD 2-8-0

90338	90388	90525	90706	90708

Total 167

Allocations: 1959 (26A)

Class 3 2-6-2T
40013   40015   44063
40014   40062   44065

Class 4 2-6-4T

42063	42288	52548	42623	42651
42287	42451	42549	42624	42660

Class 6P5F 2-6-0

42701	42707	42714	42733
42703	42708	42715	42750
42704	42709	42726	42871
42705	42710	42728	42901

Class 4F 0-6-0
44022   44311   44543

Class 5 4-6-0

44696	44933	45202	45233
44697	44934	45203	45284
44734	45031	45220	45290
44735	45076	45224	45336
44736	45101	45225	45341
44803	45102	45232	45435
44845	45103		
44890	45104		
44891	45105		
44893	45154 *Lanarkshire Yeomanry*		
44894	45156 *Ayrshire Yeomanry*		
44895			

'Patriot' 4-6-0
45509 *The Derbyshire Yeomanry*

'Jubilee' 4-6-0
45635 *Tobago*
45642 *Boscawen*
45661 *Vernon*
45700 *Amethyst*
45701 *Conqueror*
45702 *Colossus*
45706 *Express*
45710 *Irresistible*

Class 2 2-6-0
46411   46419   46484
46418   46437   46487

Looking towards the massive 24-road depot in 1939 from the coaling plant showing a variety of the classes to be found there. This was the largest shed on the LYR system.
Crown Copyright National Railway Museum

Class 3F 0-6-0T
47207	47224	47546
47217	47440	47547

Class 8F 2-8-0
48115	48372	48553	48720
48148	48491	48716	48745

Class 7F 0-8-0
49508	49515	49624
49511	49592	49667

Class 2F 0-6-0ST
51343	51371	51458	51497

Class 3F 0-6-0
52108	52161	52271	52341
52140	52230	52275	52431
52141	52270	52278	52455

Class 4 2-6-4T
80044	80060	80061

Class WD 2-8-0
90105	90245	90328	90389	90548
90142	90248	90338	90390	90576
90163	90271	90366	90523	90589
90197	90289	90376	90530	90669
90222	90291	90388	90533	90715

Class 9F 2-10-0
92015	92016	92017	92161	92162

Total 154

Class 3F 0-6-0T
47408	47480	47656	47660

Class 8F 2-8-0
48136	48331	48426	48612	48765
48318	48372	48532	48756	48775
48321	48391	48533	48758	

Class 9F 2-10-0
92016	92050	92077	92114
92018	92051	92080	92159
92022	92052	92081	92161
92026	92056	92110	92162

Total 79

26B AGECROFT

Pre-Grouping Origin: Lancashire & Yorkshire Railway
Gazetteer Ref: 45 B2
Closed: 1966
Shed-Codes: 26B (1948-1963)
9J (1963-1966)
Allocations: 1950 (26B)

Allocations: 1965 (9D)

Class 4MT 2-6-4T
42079	42115	42492	42656
42087	42464	42548	

Class 4F 0-6-0
44247

Class 5MT 4-6-0
44697	44890	45083	45255	45343
44734	44891	45101	45271	45435
44803	44933	45202	45336	
44818	44934	45203	45339	
44845	45076	45246	45341	

'Jubilee' 4-6-0
45600 Bermuda
45604 Ceylon
45705 Seahorse

Class 2MT 2-6-0
46406	46437	46501
46411	46449	46513
46412	46452	46514
46418	46485	46523

Class 4P 4-4-0
41100	41189	41191	41196

Class 4MT 2-6-4T
42645	42646	42647	42648

Class 5MT 2-6-0
42721	42724	42753	42819	42864
42722	42725	42755	42838	42868
42723	42734	42796	42860	

Class 5MT 4-6-0
44781	44782	44823	45338

Class 3F 0-6-0T
47574	47579	47584
47578	47583	47585

The depot in 1926 during the coal strike, hence the security measures! Upon closure the engines went to Bolton, Patricroft and Trafford Park. As will be seen in the diagram, the covered accommodation had been halved by 1954. A. G. Ellis

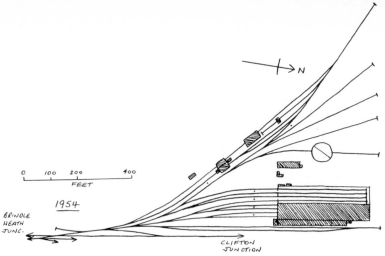

BRINDLE
HEATH
JUNC.

1954

0   100   200   400
FEET

N

CLIFTON
JUNCTION

Class 8F 2-8-0
48724   48725   48732   48760   48766
Class 7F 0-8-0
49502   49532   49544   49570   49627
49511   49538   49555   49578   49638
Class OF 0-4-0ST
51230
Class 2F 0-6-0ST
51390   51464   51500   51512
Class 3F 0-6-0
52140   52219   52279   52293

Total 56

Allocations: 1959 (26B)

Class 4 2-6-4T
42645   42646   42647
Class 6P5F 2-6-0
42723   42725   42753   42819   42860
42724   42734   42755   42838   42868
Class 5 4-6-0
44781   44929   45116   45261   45450
44782   44932   45223   45337
44823   44987   45234   45338
Class 2 2-6-0
46485   46486
Class 3F 0-6-0T
47574   47578   47579   47583   47585
Class 7F 0-8-0
49505   49509   49578   49627   49668
Class OF 0-4-0ST
51204   51207
Class 2F 0-6-0ST
51413   51496
Class WD 2-8-0
90292   90354   90546   90632
90307   90359   90558   90713
90324   90372   90564

Total 53

Allocations: 1965 (9J)

Class 5MT 4-6-0
44781   44822   44987   45368   45437
44782   44928   45096   45420
44817   44929   45133   45424

Class 3F 0-6-0T
47428
Class 8F 2-8-0
48026   48250   48535   48634
48164   48397   48536   48682
48224   48521   48539   48708

Total 26

26C   BOLTON

Pre-Grouping Origin: Lancashire & Yorkshire
Railway
Gazetteer Ref: 45 B2
Closed: 1968
Shed-Codes: 26C (1948-1963)
9K (1963-1968)
Allocations: 1950 (26C)

Class 4P 4-4-0
41085   41103   41104   41186   41190
Class 4MT 2-6-4T
42472   42565   42652   42654   42656
42545   42633   42653   42655   42657
Class 8F 2-8-0
48453   48710   48762   48767
48468   48711   48765
Class 7F 0-8-0
49510   49640   49664   49672
Class 2P 2-4-2T
50647   50807   50818   50831   50872
50660   50815   50829   50865
Class 2F 0-6-0ST
51511   51513   51519
Class 3F 0-6-0
52136   52311   52446
52212   52348
52231   52350
52236   52404

Total 47

Looking south towards the shed in 1937. Quite unlike its neighbouring depot (10D Plodder Lane) Bolton LYR shed survived into the last year of steam working, 1968. LGRP courtesy David & Charles

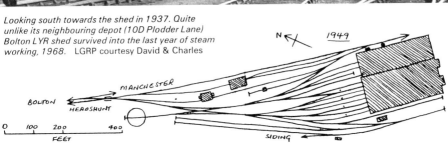

Allocations: 1959 (26C)

Class 4 2-6-4T

42289	42565	42633	42653	42656
42472	42626	42635	42654	
42545	42630	42652	42655	

Class 7F 0-8-0

49544	49618	49662	49674

Class 2P 2-4-2T
50850

Class 2F 0-6-0ST

51408	51486	51498

Class 3F 0-6-0

52348	52389	52393	52415	52523

Class 2 2-6-2T

84014	84019

Class WD 2-8-0

90102	90206	90297	90725
90110	90267	90641	90729

Total 36

Allocations: 1965 (9K)

Class 4MT 2-6-4T

42155	42249	42484	42574	42676
42183	42426	42555	42626	

Class 4F 0-6-0
44311

Class 5MT 4-6-0

44664	44893	45239	45304	45381
44728	44927	45252	45318	45409
44736	44947	45260	45351	45411
44737	45104	45290	45377	45415

Class 2MT 2-6-0

46405	46417	46504
46414	46436	46506
46416	46439	

Class 3F 0-6-0T

47388	47520

Class 8F 2-8-0

48106	48333	48495	48547	48740
48205	48371	48511	48652	48773
48295	48469	48523	48702	

Class 2MT 2-6-2T

84017	84019	84025

Total 57

26D   BURY

Pre-Grouping Origin: Lancashire & Yorkshire Railway
Gazetteer Ref: 45 B2
Closed: 1965
Shed-Codes: 26D (1948-1963)
9M (1963-1965)
Allocations: 1950 (26D)

Class 4MT 2-6-4T

42473	42474	42476	42629

Class 7F 0-8-0

49508	49591	49666
49557	49594	49667

Class 2F 0-6-0ST

51376	51419	51486	51489	51504

Class 3F 0-6-0

52129	52165	52382	52581
52159	52245	52554	52615
52164	52246	52580	

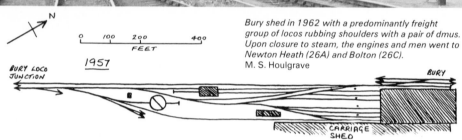

Bury shed in 1962 with a predominantly freight group of locos rubbing shoulders with a pair of dmus. Upon closure to steam, the engines and men went to Newton Heath (26A) and Bolton (26C). M. S. Houlgrave

BURY LOCO JUNCTION

1957

BURY

CARRIAGE SHED

Class WD 2-8-0
90364   90419

Total 28

Allocations: 1959 (26D)

Class 4 2-6-4T
42444   42455   42460   42550
Class 6P5F 2-6-0
42700   42719   42731
42712   42730   42820
Class 2 2-6-0
46406   46414   46416   46417   46436
Class 3F 0-6-0T
47584
Class 3F 0-6-0
52129   52289   52443   52527
Class WD 2-8-0
90194   90226   90419   90626
90205   90364   90555   90718
90219   90408   90568

Total 31

26E   BACUP

Pre-Grouping Origin: Lancashire & Yorkshire Railway
Gazetteer Ref: 20 A1
Closed: 1954
Shed-Code: 26E (1948-1954)
Allocations: 1950

Class 2P 4-4-0
40682   40691
Class 4P 2-6-4T
42619   42620   42649   42650   42651
Class 2P 2-4-2T
50651   50652
Class 3F 0-6-0
52299   52416   52440   52443

Total 13

1954

BURY

WHITWORTH

26E BACUP

A 1951 view of Bacup shed. C. A. Appleton

26F LEES

Pre-Grouping Origin: LNWR
Gazetteer Ref: 21 F1
Closed: 1964
Shed-Codes: 26F (1948-1955)
26E (1955-1963)
9P (1963-1964)

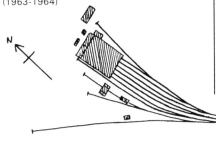

Allocations: 1950 (26F)

Class 3MT 2-6-2T
40012	40056	40059	40061
40014	40057	40060	40062

Class 7F 0-8-0
49509	49548	49590	49593	49668

Class 3F 0-6-0
52099	52365	52387	52464
52248	52378	52389	

Class WD 2-8-0
90112	90626	90720

Total 23

Allocations: 1959(26E)

Class 2 2-6-2T
41206

Class 4 2-6-4T
42114	42115	42551	42657

The shed in the late 1950s from a southerly
viewpoint. The depot had the distinction of being the
last stronghold of the 'Aspinall' Class 3F 0-6-0

freight locos before their complete withdrawal in
1961. The shed was sometimes referred to as
Oldham. Photomatic

Class 3F 0-6-0
52183	52248	52322	52466
52240	52269	52410	

Class 2 2-6-2T
84013

Class WD 2-8-0
90123	90141	90402	90671
90140	90306	90525	90708

Total 21

Class 4F 0-6-0
43927	44019	44025	44114
43952	44022	44040	44119

Class 5MT 4-6-0
44803	44921	45031	45284	45450

Class 3F 0-6-0T
47336   47440

Class 8F 2-8-0
48110	48330	48349
48188	48348	48531

Class 2F 0-6-0ST
51484

Total 32

26G   BELLE VUE

Pre-Grouping Origin: Midland Railway
Gazetteer Ref: 45 A3
Closed: 1956
Shed-Codes: 19E (1948-1949)
13B (1949)
26G (1949-1955)
26F (1955-1956)
Allocations: 1950 (26G)

Class 1F 0-6-0T
41690   41702   41814

Class 4MT 2-6-4T
42675

Class 5MT 2-6-0
42765   42898

Class 3F 0-6-0
43612   43630   43638   43756

27A   BANK HALL

Pre-Grouping Origin: Lancashire & Yorkshire Railway
Gazetteer Ref: 45 F3
Closed: 1966
Shed-Codes: 23A (1948-1950)
27A (1950-1963)
8K (1963-1966)
Allocations: 1950 (27A)

Class 2P 4-4-0
40581   40582   40584   40585

Class 4P 4-4-0
41187   41193

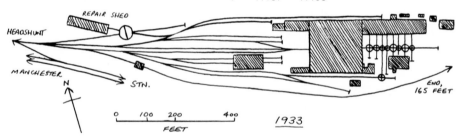

Looking east to Belle Vue in 1954 with Class 4 0-6-0 No 44486 at rest over the pits. Upon closure most of the locos went to Newton Heath (26A), but a number did find a home at the nearby Gorton (39A) shed.   H. C. Casserley

Looking north to the running shed in LMS days. This, the principal LYR depot in Liverpool, was known as 'Sandhills' prior to 1920. Upon closure the locos and men went to Aintree (27B).   A. G. Ellis

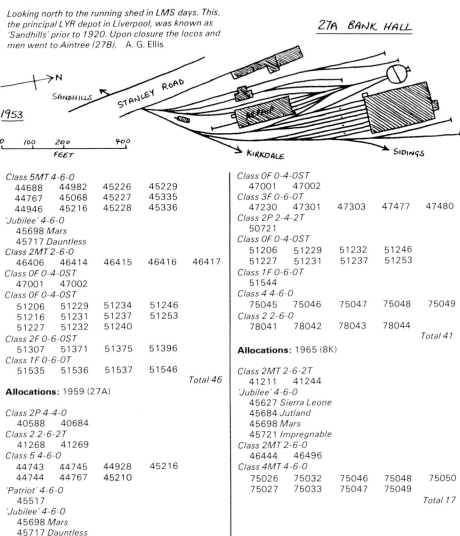

27A BANK HALL

1953

0   100   200   400
FEET

SANDHILLS
STANLEY ROAD
KIRKDALE
SIDINGS

Class 5MT 4-6-0
44688	44982	45226	45229
44767	45068	45227	45335
44946	45216	45228	45336

'Jubilee' 4-6-0
45698 *Mars*
45717 *Dauntless*

Class 2MT 2-6-0
46406	46414	46415	46416	46417

Class 0F 0-4-0ST
47001   47002

Class 0F 0-4-0ST
51206	51229	51234	51246
51216	51231	51237	51253
51227	51232	51240	

Class 2F 0-6-0ST
51307	51371	51375	51396

Class 1F 0-6-0T
51535	51536	51537	51546

Total 46

Allocations: 1959 (27A)

Class 2P 4-4-0
40588   40684

Class 2 2-6-2T
41268   41269

Class 5 4-6-0
44743	44745	44928	45216
44744	44767	45210	

'Patriot' 4-6-0
45517

'Jubilee' 4-6-0
45698 *Mars*
45717 *Dauntless*
45719 *Glorious*

Class 0F 0-4-0ST
47001   47002

Class 3F 0-6-0T
47230   47301   47303   47477   47480

Class 2P 2-4-2T
50721

Class 0F 0-4-0ST
51206	51229	51232	51246
51227	51231	51237	51253

Class 1F 0-6-0T
51544

Class 4 4-6-0
75045   75046   75047   75048   75049

Class 2 2-6-0
78041   78042   78043   78044

Total 41

Allocations: 1965 (8K)

Class 2MT 2-6-2T
41211   41244

'Jubilee' 4-6-0
45627 *Sierra Leone*
45684 *Jutland*
45698 *Mars*
45721 *Impregnable*

Class 2MT 2-6-0
46444   46496

Class 4MT 4-6-0
75026   75032   75046   75048   75050
75027   75033   75047   75049

Total 17

133

27B AINTREE

Pre-Grouping Origin: Lancashire & Yorkshire Railway
Gazetteer Ref: 45 F3
Closed: 1967
Shed-Codes: 23B (1948-1950)
27B (1950-1963)
8L (1963-1967)
Allocations: 1950 (27B)

Class 4F 0-6-0

44462	44481	44541

Class 8F 2-8-0

48515	48523	48524	48525	48713

Class 7F 0-8-0

49503	49535	49582	49609	49641
49505	49547	49586	49617	49649
49506	49552	49592	49623	49671
49515	49563	49595	49624	
49523	49566	49600	49631	
49524	49571	49603	49635	

Class 2P 2-4-2T

50648	50655

Class 2F 0-6-0

51343	51413	51460	51462	51530

Class 1F 0-6-0T

51544

Class 3F 0-6-0

52093	52196	52312	52405
52112	52218	52362	52412
52179	52244	52381	52557

Total 55

Allocations: 1959 (27B)

Class 6P5F 2-6-0

42711	42727	42864
42721	42845	42878

Class 2 2-6-0

46405	46412	46439

Class 3F 0-6-0T

47259	47305	47425

Class 7F 0-8-0

49582	49586	49640

Class 1F 0-6-0T

51537

Class 3F 0-6-0

52135	52171	52260	52311	52378

Class WD 2-8-0

90101	90278	90343	90535	90724
90107	90282	90375	90552	
90164	90283	90381	90643	
90204	90316	90416	90687	
90216	90327	90527	90712	

Total 42

Allocations: 1965 (8L)

Class 5MT 4-6-0

44958	45068	45229	45323	45330

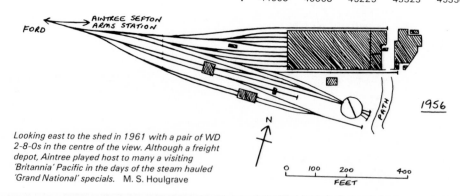

Looking east to the shed in 1961 with a pair of WD 2-8-0s in the centre of the view. Although a freight depot, Aintree played host to many a visiting 'Britannia' Pacific in the days of the steam hauled 'Grand National' specials. M. S. Houlgrave

Class 2MT 2-6-0
| 46404 | 46500 | 46502 |

Class 3F 0-6-0T
| 47289 | 47512 | 47655 |
| 47327 | 47566 | 47681 |

Class 8F 2-8-0
48017	48268	48422	48558	48704
48050	48290	48451	48605	48715
48108	48340	48465	48648	
48139	48421	48500	48676	

Class 4MT 4-6-0
| 75043 | 75060 | 75061 | 75064 |

Class WD 2-8-0
| 90222 | 90346 | 90632 | 90706 |
| 90306 | 90563 | 90641 | 90724 |

Total 44

27C SOUTHPORT

Pre-Grouping Origin: Lancashire & Yorkshire
Railway
Gazetteer Ref: 45 F1
Closed: 1966
Shed-Codes: 23C (1948-1950)
27C (1950-1963)
8M (1963-1966)
Allocations: 1950 (27C)

Class 3MT 2-6-2T
| 40190 | 40192 | 40195 | 40197 |
| 40191 | 40194 | 40196 | 40198 |

Class 4P 4-4-0
| 41102 |

Class 4MT 2-6-4T
| 42291 | 42292 | 42293 | 42294 |

Class 5MT 4-6-0
44728	44887	45061	45415
44729	44926	45200	45435
44737	44989	45334	

Class 2F 0-6-0ST
| 51490 |

Class 3F 0-6-0
| 52161 | 52162 | 52183 | 52278 | 52582 |

Total 30

Allocations: 1959 (27C)

Class 3 2-6-2T
| 40090 | 40194 | 40196 | 40198 |
| 40191 | 40195 | 40197 | 40199 |

Class 4 2-6-4T
| 42290 | 42293 | 42537 | 42637 |
| 42292 | 42435 | 42621 | |

Class 5 4-6-0
| 44728 | 44887 | 45061 | 45228 |
| 44729 | 44989 | 45218 | |

Class 2P 2-4-2T
| 50746 | 50781 |

Class 4 4-6-0
| 75015 | 75016 | 75017 | 75018 | 75019 |

Total 29

Allocations: 1965 (8M)

Class 4MT 2-6-4T
| 42061 | 42132 | 42662 |
| 42078 | 42645 | 42675 |

Class 5MT 4-6-0
| 44686 | 44687 | 44757 | 44809 | 45055 |

Total 11

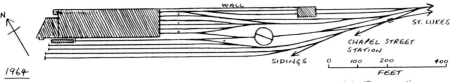

1964

The shed in 1963 looking from the turntable. In
1961 this depot boasted the last ex-LYR Class 2P
2-4-2T, No 50850 from a once very numerous class.

The shed today forms part of the 'Steamport'
Transport Museum. M. S. Houlgrave

27D　WIGAN

Pre-Grouping Origin: Lancashire & Yorkshire Railway
Gazetteer Ref: 45 D2
Closed: 1964
Shed-Codes: 23D (1948-1950)
27D (1950-1963)
8P (1963-1964)
Allocations: 1950 (27D)

Class 3MT 2-6-2T
40199
Class 2P 4-4-0
40580　40587　40678　40684
Class 4P 4-4-0
41101
Class 4MT 2-6-4T
42297　42554　42592　42632　42642
42299　42557　42614　42640　42644
42537　42569　42631　42641
Class 7F 0-8-0
49568　49585　49587　49610
Class 2F 0-6-0ST
51474

Class 3F 0-6-0
52169　52288　52379　52413　52549
52197　52360　52390　52450
Class 6F 0-8-0
52727*　52822　52831
Class 7F 0-8-0
52870　52906　52910　52916　52945
　　　　　　　　　　　　　　　　Total 42

*No 52727 became the sole survivor in 1950 and was the only one to receive its BR number.

Allocations: 1959 (27D)

Class 2P 4-4-0
40587　40680　40681
Class 4 2-6-4T
42180　42475　42592　42640
42297　42554　42614　42641
42299　42557　42631　42642
42473　42569　42632　42644
Class 4F 0-6-0
43952　44225　44464　44544
44221　44240　44486
Class 7F 0-8-0
49637
Class 2 2-6-0
78040　78061　78063
78060　78062　78064

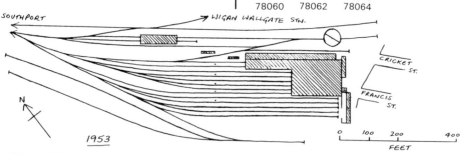

1953

This once 14-road shed was greatly diminished by BR days and of the eight covered tracks, only two had survived the original sheltered length. A view of the shed in 1951 shows No 52162 and other Class 3F 0-6-0s in the open. The depot was sometimes referred to as Wigan Central.　W. Potter

Class WD 2-8-0
90121   90561   90570   90599
Total 37

27E WALTON ON THE HILL

Pre-Grouping Origin: Cheshire Lines Railway
Gazetteer Ref: 45 F3
Closed: 1963
Shed-Codes: 13F (1949)
27E (1949-1963)
8R (1963)
Allocations: 1950 (27E)

Class 2P 4-4-0
40690
Class 4P 4-4-0
40937   41194
Class 2MT 2-6-0
46436
Class 3F 0-6-0
52271   52328   52333   52437
Class J11 0-6-0
64397
Class J10 0-6-0
65130   65133   65177   65180   65192

Classes J67 & J69* 0-6-0T
68584   68585*
Class N5 0-6-2T
69265   69298   69344   69356
Total 20
Allocations: 1959 (27E)

Class 4 2-6-4T
42112   42113
Class 4F 0-6-0
44014   44188   44299   44481
44038   44218   44462   44605
44040   44291   44471
Class 3F 0-6-0T
47225   47228   47235   47655   47681
Class J10 0-6-0
65133
Class N5 0-6-2T
69265   69298   69344
Total 22

28A BLACKPOOL CENTRAL

Pre-Grouping Origin: Lancashire & Yorkshire Railway
Gazetteer Ref: 24 D4
Closed: 1964

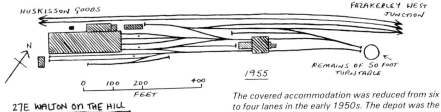

HUSKISSON GOODS

FAZAKERLEY WEST JUNCTION

N

REMAINS OF 50 FOOT TURNTABLE

1955

0   100   200   400
FEET

27E WALTON ON THE HILL

The covered accommodation was reduced from six to four lanes in the early 1950s. The depot was the only one in the country to receive a shed-code suffix as high as 'R'.   J. A. Peden

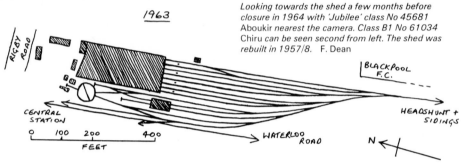

1963

Looking towards the shed a few months before closure in 1964 with 'Jubilee' class No 45681 Aboukir *nearest the camera. Class B1 No 61034* Chiru *can be seen second from left. The shed was rebuilt in 1957/8.*   F. Dean

RIGBY ROAD

BLACKPOOL F.C.

CENTRAL STATION

HEADSHUNT + SIDINGS

0   100   200   400
FEET

WATERLOO ROAD

N

Shed-Codes: 24E (1948-1950)
28A (1950-1952)
24E (1952-1963)
10B (1963-1964)
Allocations: 1950 (28A)

Class 4P 4-4-0
  41185   41192   41195
Class 4MT 2-6-4T
  42148   42636   42637   42638
Class 5MT 4-6-0
  44730   44778   44929   44950   45107
  44731   44779   44930   44988   45214
  44732   44927   44932   45043
  44733   44928   44947   45077

'Jubilee' 4-6-0
  45571 *South Africa*
  45574 *India*
  45588 *Kashmir*
  45653 *Barham*
  45695 *Minotaur*
  45697 *Achilles*
  45707 *Valiant*
Class 2MT 2-6-0
  46410   46411   46412   46413   46435
Class 5P 4-6-0
  50455
Class 2P 2-4-2T

  50721   50746   50752   50777
  50725   50749   50757
Class 3F 0-6-0
  52138   52174   52194   52240   52334
  52157   52182   52215   52275   52357

  52415   52447   52466
  52430   52459   52572

Total 61

Allocation: 1959 (24E)

Class 3 2-6-2T
  40072   40103   40164   40174
  40099   40109   40166
Class 4 2-6-4T
  42148   42461   42625   42638
Class 5 4-6-0
  44730   44737   44927   44982   45201
  44731   44778   44930   44988   45318
  44732   44779   44947   45077   45436
  44733   44926   44950   45200   45464
'Jubilee' 4-6-0
  45571 *South Africa*
  45574 *India*
  45580 *Burma*
  45584 *North West Frontier*
  45653 *Barham*
  45705 *Seahorse*
Class 4 2-6-4T
  80046   80093

Total 39

138

28B FLEETWOOD

Looking south west to the depot in 1962. Upon closure most of the engines and men transferred to Lostock Hall (24C). M. S. Houlgrave

Pre-Grouping Origin: Lancashire & Yorkshire Railway
Gazetteer Ref: 24 C4
Closed: 1966
Shed-Codes: 24F (1948-1950)
28B (1950-1952)
24F (1952-1963)
10C (1963-1966)
Allocations: 1950 (28B)

Class 2MT 2-6-2T
| 41260 | 41261 | 41262 | 41263 | 41264 |

Class 5MT 2-6-0
| 42729 | 42841 | 42844 |
| 42840 | 42842 | 42867 |

Class 5MT 4-6-0
| 44948 | 45212 |

Class 2F 0-6-0T
| 47161 | 47165 |

Class 2P 2-4-2T
50640	50720	50781	50840
50642	50766	50802	50850
50646	50778	50812

Class 2F 0-6-0ST
| 51321 | 51477 | 51481 | 51498 |

Class 3F 0-6-0
| 52290 | 52458 | 52588 |

Total 33

Allocations: 1959 (24F)

Class 2 2-6-2T
| 41205 | 41260 | 41261 | 41283 |

Class 6P5F 2-6-0
| 42732 | 42840 | 42842 | 42844 |
| 42765 | 42841 | 42843 | 42867 |

Class 5 4-6-0
| 45107 | 45206 | 45212 |

Class 2F 0-6-0T
| 47161 | 47165 |

Class 2F 0-6-0ST
| 51336 | 51419 | 51524 |

Class 2 2-6-2T
| 84016 | 84017 | 84018 |

Total 23

Allocations: 1965 (10C)

Class 4MT 2-6-4T
| 42460 | 42494 |

Class 5MT 4-6-0
44675	44988	45206	45421
44729	45107	45274	45444
44982	45200	45347

Class 3F 0-6-0T
| 47317 | 47666 |

Class 8F 2-8-0
| 48099 | 48211 | 48319 | 48413 |
| 48199 | 48223 | 48377 | 48618 |

Class 2MT 2-6-2T
| 84010 | 84016 |

Total 25

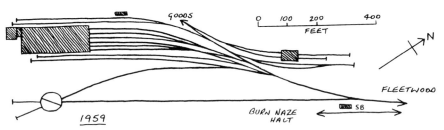

29C DUNDEE WEST

The depot in 1954 from an eastern viewpoint. A boarded crossing led to the nearby ex-NB Tay Bridge depot standing to the east of its ex-Caledonian counterpart. Photomatic

Pre-Grouping Origin: Caledonian Railway
Gazetteer Ref: 34 E4
Closed: 1958
Shed-Code: 29C (1948-1949)
Allocation: 1945 (LMS 29C) (Eventual BR numbers in brackets)

Class 2P 0-4-4T
  15173 (55173)
  15180* (none)
  15186 (55186)
  15196* (55196)
  15223 (55223)
  15226 (55226)
  15231 (55231)
Class 3 F 0-6-0T
  16323 (56323)
  16325 (56325)
Class 2F 0-6-0
  17450* (57450)
Class 3F 0-6-0
  17568 (57568)
  17653 (57653)

Total 12

Although not officially closed as a running depot until 1951, no definite allocation under BR has been traced. However, of the above locos all except those marked were part of the official 1950 Dundee Tay Bridge (62B Scottish Region) allocation, under which Dundee West served as a sub-shed until complete closure in 1958. It can therefore be assumed that these engines formed the majority of Dundee West's working allocation until 1951.

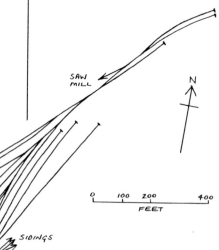

1954

SAW MILL

N

SIDINGS

DUNDEE WEST STN.

BUCKINGHAM WEST JUNCTION

0   100   200   400
      FEET

Between 1951 and closure the depot merely repaired and stored locomotives from the cramped Tay Bridge shed. Examples of motive power to be found at Dundee West in 1956 for example were: (All 62B coded unless otherwise stated) Nos 42691, 45486, 55227, 60804, 60844, 60969, 60971, 61180, 62434 *Kettledrummle*, 64530, 64613 (64A), 64620, 65907 (62A), 67484, 68123, 68551, 90198, 90463, 90515. Upon closure the shed was refitted for use as a diesel depot.

List of Shed-Codes

The following list sets out every shed-code that existed for steam Motive Power Depots under the London Midland Region from 1948 to 1968 along with each venue and its length of occupancy.

1A	Willesden 1948-65
1B	Camden 1948-61
1C	Watford 1948-65
1D	Devons Road 1949-58
1E	Bletchley 1952-65
1F	Rugby 1963-65
1G	Woodford Halse 1963-65
1H	Northampton 1963-65

2A	Rugby 1948-63. Tyseley 1963-66
2B	Bletchley 1948-50. Nuneaton 1950-63. Oxley 1963-67
2C	Northampton 1948-50. Warwick 1950-58. Stourbridge 1963-66
2D	Nuneaton 1948-50. Coventry 1950-59. Banbury 1963-66
2E	Warwick 1948-50. Northampton 1952-63. Saltley 1963-67
2F	Coventry 1948-50. Market Harborough 1955-58. Woodford Halse 1958-63. Bescot 1963-66
2G	Woodford Halse 1958
2J	Aston 1963-65
2K	Bushbury 1963-65
2L	Leamington Spa 1963-65
2M	Wellington 1963-64
2P	Kidderminster 1963-64

3A	Bescot 1948-60
3B	Bushbury 1948-60
3C	Walsall 1948-58
3D	Aston 1948-60
3E	Monument Lane 1948-60

4A	Shrewsbury 1948-49. Bletchley 1950-52
4B	Swansea Victoria 1948-49. Northampton 1950-52
4C	Upper Bank 1948-49
4D	Abergavenny 1948-49
4E	Tredegar 1948-49

5A	Crewe North 1948-65
5B	Crewe South 1948-67
5C	Stafford 1948-65
5D	Stoke 1948-67
5E	Alsager 1948-62. Nuneaton 1963-66
5F	Uttoxeter 1948-64

6A	Chester LNWR 1948-67
6B	Mold Junction 1948-66
6C	Birkenhead 1948-63. Croes Newydd 1963-67
6D	Northgate 1949-60. Shrewsbury 1963-67
6E	Rhosddu 1949-58. Chester (GWR) 1958-60. Oswestry 1963-65
6F	Bidston 1949-63. Machynlleth 1963-66
6G	Llandudno Junction 1952-66

6H	Bangor 1952-65
6J	Holyhead 1952-66
6K	Rhyl 1952-63

7A	Llandudno Junction 1948-52
7B	Bangor 1948-52
7C	Holyhead 1948-52
7D	Rhyl 1948-52

8A	Edge Hill 1948-68
8B	Warrington Dallam 1948-67
8C	Speke Junction 1948-68
8D	Widnes 1948-64
8E	Brunswick 1950-58. Northwich 1958-68
8F	Springs Branch 1958-67
8G	Sutton Oak 1958-67
8H	Birkenhead 1963-67
8K	Bank Hall 1963-66
8L	Aintree 1963-67
8M	Southport 1963-66
8P	Wigan LYR 1963-64
8R	Walton on the Hill 1963

9A	Longsight 1948-65
9B	Stockport 1948-68
9C	Macclesfield 1948-61
9D	Buxton 1948-63. Newton Heath 1963-68
9E	Trafford Park 1950-56 & 1958-68
9F	Heaton Mersey 1950-56 & 1958-68
9G	Northwich 1950-58. Gorton 1958-65
9H	Gorton 1958. Patricroft 1963-68
9J	Agecroft 1963-65
9K	Bolton 1963-68
9L	Buxton 1963-68
9M	Bury 1963-65
9P	Lees 1963-64

10A	Springs Branch 1948-58. Carnforth 1963-68
10B	Preston 1948-58. Blackpool 1963-64.
10C	Patricroft 1948-58. Fleetwood 1963-66
10D	Plodder Lane 1948-54. Sutton Oak 1955-58. Lostock Hall 1963-68
10E	Sutton Oak 1948-55
10F	Wigan Lower Ince 1950-52. Rose Grove 1963-68
10G	Skipton 1963-67
10H	Lower Darwen 1963-66
10J	Lancaster 1963-66

11A	Carnforth 1948-58. Barrow 1958-60
11B	Barrow 1948-58. Workington 1958-60
11C	Oxenholme 1950-60
11D	Oxenholme 1948-50. Tebay 1950-60
11E	Tebay 1948-50. Lancaster 1951-57

12A	Kingmoor 1948-49. Upperby 1950-58. Kingmoor 1958-68
12B	Upperby 1948-50. Canal 1950-51. Penrith 1955-58. Upperby 1958-66
12C	Penrith 1948-55. Workington 1955-58. Canal 1958-63. Barrow 1963-66
12D	Workington 1948-55. Canal 1958. Kirkby Stephen 1958-61. Workington 1963-68
12E	Moor Row 1948-54. Kirkby Stephen 1958. Barrow 1960-63. Tebay 1963-68
12F	Beattock 1948-49. Workington 1960-63
12G	Dumfries 1948-49. Oxenholme 1960-62
12H	Stranraer 1948-49. Tebay 1960-63

13A	Plaistow 1948-49. Trafford Park 1949-50	
13B	Devons Road 1948-49. Belle Vue 1949-50	
13C	Tilbury 1948-49. Heaton Mersey 1949-50	
13D	Shoeburyness 1948-49. Northwich 1949-50	
13E	Upminster 1948-49. Brunswick 1949-50	
13F	Walton on the Hill 1949-50	
13G	Wigan Lower Ince 1949-50	
14A	Cricklewood 1948-63	
14B	Kentish Town 1948-63. Cricklewood 1963-64	
14C	St Albans 1948-60. Bedford 1963	
14D	Neasden 1958-62	
14E	Bedford 1958-63	
15A	Wellingborough 1948-63. Leicester (MR) 1963-66	
15B	Kettering 1948-63. Wellingborough 1963-66	
15C	Leicester (MR) 1948-63. Kettering 1963-65	
15D	Bedford 1948-58. Coalville 1958-63. Leicester (GCR) 1963-64	
15E	Leicester (GCR) 1958-63. Coalville 1963-65	
15F	Market Harborough 1958-60	
16A	Nottingham 1948-63. Toton 1963-65	
16B	Pet. Spital Bridge 1948-50. Kirkby in Ashfield 1955-63. Annesley 1963-66. Colwick 1966	
16C	Kirkby in Ashfield 1948-55. Mansfield 1955-60. Derby 1963-67	
16D	Mansfield 1948-55. Annesley 1958-63. Nottingham 1963-65	
16E	Kirkby in Ashfield 1963-66	
16F	Burton 1963-66	
16G	Westhouses 1963-66	
16H	Hasland 1963-64	
16J	Rowsley 1963-64	
17A	Derby 1948-63	
17B	Burton 1948-63	
17C	Coalville 1948-58. Rowsley 1958-63	
17D	Rowsley 1948-58	
17E	Heaton Mersey 1957-58	
17F	Trafford Park 1957-58	
18A	Toton 1948-63	
18B	Westhouses 1948-63	
18C	Hasland 1948-63	
18D	Staveley MR 1948-58	
19A	Grimesthorpe 1948-58	
19B	Millhouses 1948-58	
19C	Canklow 1948-58	
19D	Heaton Mersey 1948-49	
19E	Belle Vue 1948-49	
19F	Trafford Park 1948-49	
20A	Holbeck 1948-57	
20B	Stourton 1948-57	
20C	Royston 1948-57	
20D	Normanton 1948-57	
20E	Manningham 1948-57	
20F	Skipton 1948-50 & 1951-57	
20G	Hellifield 1948-50 & 1951-57	
20H	Lancaster 1948-50	
21A	Saltley 1948-63	
21B	Bourneville 1948-60. Bescot 1960-63	

21C	Bromsgrove 1948-58. Bushbury 1960-63
21D	Stratford on Avon 1948-53. Aston 1960-63
21E	Monument Lane 1960-62
22A	Barrow Road 1948-58
22B	Gloucester Barnwood 1948-58
22C	Bath Green Park 1948-50
22D	Templecombe 1948-50
22E	Highbridge 1948-50
23A	Bank Hall 1948-50. Skipton 1950-51
23B	Aintree 1948-50. Hellifield 1950-51
23C	Southport 1948-50. Lancaster 1950-51
23D	Wigan (LYR) 1948-50
24A	Accrington 1948-61
24B	Rose Grove 1948-63
24C	Lostock Hall 1948-63
24D	Lower Darwen 1948-63
24E	Blackpool 1948-50 & 1952-63
24F	Fleetwood 1948-50 & 1952-63
24G	Skipton 1957-63
24H	Hellifield 1957-63
24J	Lancaster 1957-63
24K	Preston 1958-61
24L	Carnforth 1958-63
25A	Wakefield 1948-56
25B	Huddersfield 1948-56
25C	Goole 1948-56
25D	Mirfield 1948-56
25E	Sowerby Bridge 1948-56
25F	Low Moor 1948-56
25G	Farnley Junction 1948-56
26A	Newton Heath 1948-63
26B	Agecroft 1948-63
26C	Bolton 1948-63
26D	Bury 1948-63
26E	Bacup 1948-54. Lees 1955-63
26F	Lees 1948-55. Belle Vue 1955-56. Patricroft 1958-63
26G	Belle Vue 1950-55
27A	Polmadie 1948-49. Bank Hall 1950-63
27B	Greenock Ladyburn 1948-49. Aintree 1950-63
27C	Hamilton 1948-49. Southport 1950-63
27D	Wigan (LYR) 1950-63
27E	Walton on the Hill 1950-63
27F	Brunswick 1958-61
28A	Motherwell 1948-49. Blackpool 1950-52
28B	Dalry Road 1948-49. Fleetwood 1950-52
28C	Carstairs 1948-49
29A	Perth 1948-49
29B	Ferryhill 1948-49
29C	Dundee West 1948-49
29D	Forfar 1948-49
30A	Corkerhill* 1948-49
30B	Hurlford* 1948-49
30C	Ardrossan* 1948-49
30D	Ayr* 1948-49

31A St Rollox* 1948-49
31B Stirling* 1948-49
31C Oban* 1948-49
31D Grangemouth* 1948-49
31E Dawsholm* 1948-49

32A Inverness* 1948-49
32B Aviemore* 1948-49
32C Forres* 1948-49

*Codes to Eastern Region in 1949.

Shed-Permits

Before a motive power depot could be visited officially, written approval had to be obtained from the appropriate department of British Railways, usually the District Passenger Manager or the Public Relations Officer. This was not always forthcoming as favour was given to organised parties of 10 or more and of a minimum age of 16 years. Notwithstanding this certain depots could only be toured when the attendance of visitors was least likely to impede the work of shed-staff, ie: at weekends. In 1949 it was reported that a total of 49,736 people visited London Midland Region depots, the most popular being Willesden, Cricklewood and Kentish Town with 20,389 between them. One cannot imagine what the actual figure was as it would have been impossible to record all the 'unofficial' visits!

Permit No. 9677

BRITISH RAILWAYS BOARD
BRITISH RAILWAYS
B.R. 19141/1

Your Reference
Our Reference PV 256 KS/SB

Public Relations & ....21st October,............19...65
Publicity Officer
York.

Dear Sir,

In accordance with your request, I have been pleased to arrange for your visit(s) to Motive Power Depot(s) as shewn below, and I hope you have an instructive and enjoyable visit.

On arrival at the Depot, this letter should be presented immediately at the Depot office and a responsible member of the staff will conduct you round.

In the interests of safety, no person under 16 years of age will be allowed to visit a Motive Power Depot unless accompanied by an adult, and the visit must finish before dark. The only luggage allowed in the Motive Power Depot will be cameras, and photographs may be taken for private collection only.

Yours faithfully,

G. S. KNOX

Motive Power Depot to be visited	Date	Time	No. of Persons
Holbeck	Sat.16.7.66	11.30 a.m.	
Stourton	"	1.0 p.m.	732
Farnley Junction	"	2.30 p.m.	
Neville Hill	"	4.0 p.m.	

To :—   M. Whittle, Esq.,

Bomber Bridge,
Nr. Preston,

Index